LEARNING LESSONS

*Social Organization
in the Classroom*

Hugh Mehan

Harvard University Press
Cambridge, Massachusetts
and London, England
1979

Copyright © 1979 by the President
and Fellows of Harvard College

Library of Congress Cataloging in Publication Data

Mehan, Hugh, 1941-
    Learning lessons

    Bibliography: p.
    Includes index.
    1. Lesson planning. 2. Students—Conduct of life
3. Educational sociology. I. Title.
LB1027.M376   372.1'3   78-24298
ISBN 0-674-52015-7

To the learners in room 24

FOREWORD

I write this foreword to *Learning Lessons* from the bi-focal perspective of both long-standing colleague of the author and, for the ten months described in this book, the subject of his research. I am the classroom teacher who taught these lessons. As Hugh ("Bud") Mehan says in his introduction, I went to teach in San Diego in 1974-75 in order to make this collaboration possible. Because our collaboration is somewhat unusual, a longer story should be told.

Bud and I met in Berkeley in 1968, when we were both participants in an interdisciplinary summer-long seminar entitled "Language, Society, and the Child." During that summer, I had my first exposure to the behavioral science called ethnomethodology. I became intrigued by the new insights it might yield into classroom life, and I was impressed by Bud as one of its clearest thinkers and writers. We kept in touch while he finished his doctoral thesis (since reported in Cicourel et al., 1974) and when he settled in San Diego as director of the Teacher Education Program at UCSD. When I decided to spend a year's leave from the Harvard Graduate School of Education back in a primary classroom, I wanted someone to be there looking over my shoulder, and I knew that Bud would be an ideal observer. A couple of years and many negotiations later, that collaboration came to pass, and this book is one of the results.

During the 1974-75 school year, Bud, two of his graduate students, my co-teacher, LaDonna Coles, and I met regularly one evening a week to talk about life in our classroom and look at the videotapes that Bud had made. During those meetings, he presented his beginning analyses of the early lessons, but I was so preoccupied with thoughts of the next day that I don't think I paid much attention. The next year, back at Harvard, I put my copies of the videotapes on a high shelf and became immersed in my normal university routine. It wasn't until well into the winter, when a small group working on classroom research assembled informally at UCSD, that I got mentally reinvolved with Bud's analysis.

At that point, as I remember it, he had worked out what is now the first part of chapter 2: the two- and three-part sequences of teacher initiation, child response, and (sometimes) teacher evaluation. The more I thought about that structural description, the more incomplete it seemed. If it was the whole story, one could assemble those sequences in any order; clearly, in terms of topic, that wasn't true. Moreover, there was a question on the table from Jeffrey Shultz (now at the University of Cincinnati) about why an evaluation component was sometimes present and sometimes not. While in San Diego, I borrowed a transcript of one of the lessons (Birthplaces) and a large scroll of paper, and tried my hand at an analysis of these lessons for the first (and only) time. When we reassembled the next day, I had a glimmer, on a very messy chart, of larger structures, longer sequences of talk that started with markers in the teacher's speech like "Now" and ended eventually with an evaluation but only after the initiation received its appropriate response. Then I went back to Harvard. When Bud and I met the next time, later that same spring, he had the rest of chapter 2 all worked out—extended sequences and topically related sets—all far more elegant than I had dared to imagine.

The final picture of this hierarchical organization rings very true to me. But, in Bud's kind of research, proof of the validity of this analysis rests completely on behavioral evidence visible and audible on the videotapes: regularities in the talk, such as when evaluations occur; co-occurring changes in interactional features like posture and pace; the occurrence of procedural talk at certain junctures and not at others. My original hunch is now completely irrelevant. How important it was heuristically in the discovery—as opposed to the proof—is harder to say. I think Bud would have found those larger units anyway—because he would have been driven by his commitment to a comprehensive analysis to find an explanation for seeming irregularities in the analysis up to that point, and because non-Markovian structures that extend contingency relationships across nonadjacent units were as familiar to him from the sociological concept of reflexive tying as they were to me from transformational grammar.

In a funny way, the more elegant the analysis, the more unreal it seems to a participant. Where the researcher sees order, the participant may have felt impending chaos—especially this participant, who felt so rusty as a primary school teacher. If school is a performance, then here the main character kept thinking she'd forgotten her lines, and there was no prompter in the wings on whom to rely for help. So to me as the teacher, the psychologically most compelling part of this book—a part I never saw until it was finished—is the section in chapter 3 about the twenty-nine anomalous cases: the sequences of talk that don't fit the descriptive system, the times when the children talk out of turn or no one answers at all. In Bud's words, the teacher's "improvisational strategies" at such moments can be categorized as instances of Doing Nothing, Getting Through, Accepting the Unexpected, and Opening the Floor. Great titles—especially Getting Through. That's what teaching is; the hard core, the bottom line—whatever else happens, one somehow has to Get Through. No one else has told this part of the story quite so well.

This whole book is about just one kind of speech event—teacher-led lessons. They constitute only one out of many different kinds of speech events in a primary school day, and one with which I was initially not much concerned. My own interest in going to San Diego was less in the talk of the teacher than in the talk of the children. That interest is one of the reasons I've spent more time with the videotapes made with wireless microphones, which catch children's talk in speech events that overhead microphones never hear. (Carrasco et al., in press, and Cazden et al., in press, report these analyses.) That interest is also why it is especially gratifying to see documentation in chapter 4 that, even within the constraints of the lesson structure, children's participation increased in quantity and quality over the course of the year.

Just as a description of language (a grammar) asserts hypotheses about what the speaker of a language must learn, so a description of a lesson asserts hypotheses about what children must learn in order to participate fully and be judged as competent students. Mehan shows that, over time, in this classroom, children became more effective in responding appropriately (in timing and form) as well as correctly (in content) to the teacher's questions. They were less frequently negatively sanctioned for saying the wrong thing at the wrong time; and they became more and more successful in initiating sequences of interaction themselves. That is, they gained tacit understanding of the structure of these lessons, and they learned to function within the structure for their purposes as well as the teacher's. Since none of the participants, not even the teacher, knew this structure explicitly, the children had to learn it as they learn language, without explicit tuition. As with language, they learned more than anyone could have explicitly taught. This is the kind of subtle progress during the year that a teacher can rarely hear for herself.

But now I have an increased sense of the importance of understanding these lessons for their own sake. The focus on them in classroom interaction research, new as well as old, may have been initially influenced by their greater audibility to human observers or overhead microphones; during lessons teachers and children talk up, and they talk (pretty much) one at a time. Without wireless microphones other classroom speech events are as hard to overhear as talk at tables in a restaurant or library. But it now seems to me that justification for the attention to lessons goes beyond the artifacts of technological constraints. In any institution, one or a few speech events probably are considered by participants to be the heart of life in that institution. In many families, the heart would be the gathering at meals. In most public classrooms, the heart, at least to the teacher, would be the lessons. To the teacher, the kind of talk that goes on in these lessons may have special significance as the epitome of enacting the teaching role. (Which may be why some teachers have a hard time shifting, even if they want to, to a more "open" or "informal" classroom structure: the time spent teaching lessons is reduced, and it's harder to feel you've really been a teacher at the end of a more informal day.) To the researcher, lesson talk is probably the focal instance, the enactment of the central tendency, of the larger category of classroom talk.

This whole book is also limited to lessons in a single classroom and a somewhat special classroom at that. Arguing for one's own ordinariness is seldom very effective, and being in a position to make that argument in book form somewhat undermines the attempt. Fortunately, another research project that adds considerably to the general picture has now been finished at the Center for Applied Linguistics (CAL) in Washington. Bud refers to this work in chapter 5, but because generalizability may be a serious question to many readers, it may be useful to say more about the relationship between the products of the two efforts.

The CAL study got under way after ours and was substantially more ambitious. They were taping a year later, and ended up with more than 400 videotapes of eight classrooms, nursery through grade 3. Because of the scope of their work, it is not surprising that Mehan's analysis was finished while theirs was still in progress, and that they therefore drew on his work. The largest single section of the CAL final report, entitled "Talk and Task at Lesson Time" (Griffin and Humphrey, 1978), is about ten lessons in two kindergartens. Despite many interesting and important differences in detail, in their words, "Our view of classroom discourse is closely related to that described by Mehan; in fact, our analyses can be seen as a closer examination of various phenomena located in his research." This replication of the structural analysis of classroom talk (not necessarily its numerical frequencies) is all the more impressive because Griffin and Humphrey are sociolinguists, not sociologists, and because of demographic differences in the two sites. Whereas this book is about lessons in a public school, mixed grades 1-3, in the poorest section of San Diego, with no Anglo child in the class, the CAL project took place in an upper-class private school in the Washington, D.C., area. (Teacher differences are harder to specify. I know nothing about the two kindergarten teachers except that they too are female; and I wouldn't know what else to report as relevant here even if I knew much more.) Again in Griffin and Humphrey's words, "The similarities must emerge from similarities of classroom talk, since the age and ethnicity of the pupils and the theoretical bases diverge so much."

At least in the near future, progress toward greater generalizability in classroom research will be made, as it has been made in child language research, by the accumulation of intensive case studies of one or a small number of classrooms. Also as in child language research, it seems heuristically advantageous to search for commonalities in structure across different classrooms first. Later, from that base, we can try to understand differences—where they appear, and what effects they have on the children who participate in them. But in one important respect classroom research is happily different from child language research and from the work by the same group of researchers (as in Snow and Ferguson, 1977) on family talk to young children: classroom research is not as limited to describing the lives of middle-class children in or near university communities. One of my many deep thanks to Bud Mehan is for arranging our work to make that diversity possible.

Courtney B. Cazden

October 1978
Center for Advanced Study in the Behavioral Sciences
Stanford, California

ACKNOWLEDGMENTS

The research reported here is the result of a unique collaborative effort. It involves a considerable number of people who are interconnected in a complex web of relationships.

In the center are Courtney B. Cazden, a noted authority on child language and education, who wanted to experience once again the "real world of teaching"; her co-teacher, LaDonna Coles; and their group of energetic and vibrant students.

Cazden took a leave from the Harvard Graduate School of Education to spend a year as an elementary school teacher. She elected to teach in San Diego in order to make this collaboration possible. She taught in a cross-age, ethnically mixed classroom in an elementary school in the San Diego Unified School District. Cazden assumed full teaching responsibilities: she designed curricula, conducted lessons, evaluated students, met with parents, and attended faculty meetings.

When the aide assigned to Cazden's classroom was removed because of budgetary cutbacks in the local Follow Through program, LaDonna Coles, who holds an elementary teaching credential from the University of California, San Diego (UCSD) Teacher Education Program, joined Cazden as a team teacher in December.

This interactional network was observed and classroom activity with Cazden was videotaped regularly by my research associates, Sue Fisher and Nick Maroules, and myself. This group of researchers and teachers formed a close working relationship. We met regularly during the year to discuss observations, review videotapes, and discuss student progress, educational curricula, and classroom organization.

Fisher and Maroules did not play the subsidiary role typically associated with graduate students on a research project. They were colleagues and collaborators, not data collectors and camera operators. We worked side by side. They contributed important ideas, influenced the research process in significant ways (for example, they assisted in developing the scheme of analysis), worked on retrieval strategies and transcript assembly, and provided penetrating criticism of the written result. As Fisher and Maroules continue their investigations of the sociology of medicine and law respectively, they are continuing in the community of scholarship we began here.

This research has been directly influenced and assisted by friends and colleagues doing similar work, notably Michael Cole, William Hall, and R. P. McDermott at Rockefeller University, Frederick Erickson and Jeffrey Shultz at Harvard University, School of Education, and Peg Griffin and Roger Shuy at the Center for Applied Linguistics. This group of SHLEPPERS had managed to meet a number of times under various auspices to watch tapes, generate ideas, and share findings. These meetings have been characterized by a rare degree of cooperation and generosity. While I have tried to cite their specific contributions, my indebtedness goes beyond footnotes. At UCSD, Aaron V. Cicourel, Sam Edward Combs, Paula Levin, Lee Meihls, Patricia Worden, and especially Margaret Riel and Jürgen Streeck have been helpful in providing suggestions on draft chapters.

The project was made possible by a grant from the Ford Foundation. The support of Marge Martus for this and other unusual research projects is gratefully acknowledged. The assistance of George Mandler, who made the good offices of the Center for Human Information Processing (CHIP) available to us, is also appreciated.

The choice of the particular San Diego school was influenced by a well-established working relationship that had developed between UCSD and the school's principal and teachers. This school had been a field site for the UCSD

Teacher Education Program for three years before our project began. The close ties developed between the university and the school facilitated the introduction and maintenance of the project. The special efforts of Robert Matthews and the principal and staff of the school (who, unfortunately, must go nameless) are gratefully acknowledged.

Once again, Colleen Carpenter typed the final manuscript expertly. Her concern for quality enhanced the work immeasurably. Norma Allison completed the difficult task of indexing efficiently and competently.

CONTENTS

LEARNING LESSONS

1 LOOKING INSIDE SCHOOLS

THE ROLE OF education in American society continues to be debated by social scientists, educators, and parents. Some current topics of debate include whether the number of years of schooling influences a person's subsequent economic success, whether attending school affects intellectual processes, and whether desegregating schools reduces inequality between the races. The study reported here examines the social organization of interaction in an elementary school classroom across a school year. The structure of classroom lessons and the interactional activities of teachers and students that assemble lessons as socially organized events are described here. This description shows how the teaching-learning process unfolds in naturally occurring school situations and provides the parameters for the socialization of students into the classroom community.

A detailed examination of interaction from one classroom contrasts sharply with the prevailing approach to the study of schooling, namely, large-scale comparisons of many different schools (see, for example, Coleman et al., 1966; Sewell, Haller, and Portes, 1969; Jencks et al., 1972; Mayeske, 1973). In fact, the approach used here may seem anomalous at first. The social organization of teacher-student interaction seems to be such a "tiny" phenomenon, while there seem to be so many massive issues facing the schools: problems like school desegregation, declining literacy, equality of educational opportunity, and the like. Because the sociological and educational relevance of a study of a single classroom may not be obvious at first, I devote the first part of this chapter to

1

suggesting why it might be important to spend less time cal-
culating the long-term effects of schools on pupils and, instead, to spend more time making careful descriptions of
what takes place inside schools. After that discussion, I place
the research strategy used in this study in the context of
others that have been used to look inside schools. Finally, I
explain the policies guiding the research reported here and
the data collection and analysis procedures.

Comparing Differences between Schools and Examining the Internal Life of Schools

Correlational studies have been the predominant research
strategy in the study of the school. Correlational studies
adopt an input-output research design. Aspects of people's
lives, their social and historical contexts, are treated as social
and cognitive "factors" or variables in this design. Some factors, like the social class, age, and sex of teachers, the ability
of students, the attitudes of teachers, the size of classrooms,
are treated as input variables. Other factors, like pupil
achievement, economic opportunity, and subsequent career
patterns, are treated as output variables. The research task of
correlational studies is to test the strength of the relationship
between the input and output variables.

Educational research using the correlational model has
been especially concerned with the effect of schools on students. School effects have been measured by focusing on the
input factors that influence educational outcomes. Input
factors (that is, independent variables) include the characteristics of students' families, the characteristics of different
schools, and the intellectual endowments of students when
they first enter school. Output variables (that is, dependent
variables) include the cognitive achievement of students,
subsequent career plans, or actual occupational attainment
or job earnings.

DO SCHOOLS MAKE A DIFFERENCE?   A number of positions have been adopted concerning the influence of schooling. There has long been a liberal political and educational
ideology in this country that insists that people's chances for

success in life are not constrained by their genetically provided endowments. Instead, the tenets of this ideology are that differences in economic attainment and scholastic achievement are primarily the result of environmental influences.

The origins of this perspective may be in the British empiricists' insistence that the mind at birth is a *tabla rasa*, waiting to be etched with environmentally provided information. The most extreme form of this view in modern times is Skinner's behaviorism, which minimizes the influence of internal mechanisms in learning and maximizes the influence of environmentally provided reinforcement. Social mobility studies (Blau and Duncan, 1967; Duncan, Featherman, and Duncan, 1972; Sewell, Haller, and Portes, 1969) that conclude that years of education influence occupational status provide support for this ideology.

This ideology also gave sustenance to the compulsory education movement in the last century. More recently, the development of Head Start, Follow Through, and other compensatory educational programs was predicated on this belief. Proponents of compensatory education, at elementary, secondary, and collegiate levels, reasoned that enriching educational environments would equalize the effects of education on students deprived of stimulating home conditions.

Faith in this commitment has been shaken recently. One challenge comes from those who contend that schooling merely recapitulates the existing system of class relationships in America (Bowles and Gintes, 1976). A second challenge comes from those who emphasize the role of heredity over environment in life chances. Proponents of this position (most recently, Jensen, 1969; Herrnstein, 1971) argue that genetic factors are the most important determinants of intellectual growth. Like a hothouse, the enrichment of environment may speed the rate of growth, but the final product of growth will not exceed genetically programmed capabilities. Yet another challenge comes from those educational researchers who emphasize the role of early childhood experiences over that of school experiences in determining life chances. Comparing long-term effects of schooling on students, some researchers (notably Coleman et al., 1966) have concluded that the quality of schools has little influence on a student's achievement. Instead, they say, educational and economic opportunities seem to be most influenced by the early childhood experiences associated with the social background of students when they enter school.

The political correlates of these positions are clear, and they are similar. Each minimizes the school, albeit for different reasons. One policy inference drawn from these positions is that there is no reason to spend money on schools because the quality of schooling does not affect economic or status attainment. The geneticist position is the most extreme on this point. Its proponents claim that *no* environmental intervention, in or out of school, will make a significant difference in status attainment. The early childhood position is less extreme but still minimizes the role of schooling. Its supporters recommend emphasizing early childhood experiences, not school experiences, to equalize educational and economic opportunities. The latter position, incidentally, is the one held by proponents of early childhood education programs, including Head Start. Finally, the radical economic position also minimizes the school while arguing in favor of economic redistribution and social reorganization as the only sure means of achieving equality.

A METHODOLOGICAL IRONY Caution must be exercised, however, before we dismiss the influence of schooling, blame schools for recapitulating the class structure, or congratulate them for opening up opportunities for mobility. There is a methodological irony in the work of researchers who are debating the influence of schools on students. Although schooling is a major variable in the equation that links people's backgrounds and biographies to their success in later life, the process of education has not been examined directly by researchers who study the influence of schooling.

While schooling is recognized as an intervening process between background social context and later economic and academic attainment, the school has been treated as a "black box" in between input and output factors. *Indices* of schooling have been examined, such as the number of books in the school library, the amount of equipment in science laboratories, the opinions of teachers and administrators toward the school. But what actually happens inside schools, in classrooms, in educational testing situations, at recess, in lunchrooms, in teachers' lounges, on a practical everyday basis has not been examined by the researchers who debate the influence of schools.

This point can be made more clearly by referring specifically to the work of Jencks and his colleagues. Jencks et al. (1972) presented a finding that is essentially counterintuitive when they reported that differences in the quality of education did not lead to corresponding differences in educational outputs. Their findings ran counter to conventional wisdom: "everybody knows" that lowering student-teacher ratios, providing better books, teachers, and laboratory equipment should increase the quality of education.

Why were Jencks and his associates unable to find a relationship between the quality of education and educational attainment? I suggest that the answer to this question can be found in the nature of their methodology.

Because Jencks and his colleagues gathered their data through large-scale surveys, they could not measure the influence of such factors directly. As a result, critics of Jencks, people who fear the consequences of his conclusions, either try to reanalyze his data by manipulating the same indices of educational quality in different ways, or fall back on personal experiences, anecdotes, or intuitions to counter his arguments.

What are lacking in most discussions of the influence of schools are descriptions of the actual processes of education. If we want to know whether student-teacher ratios, classroom size, teaching styles, and all the rest actually influence the quality of education, then we must be able to show how they operate in pragmatic educational situations. Likewise, if we are to understand how so-called input factors like social class, ethnicity, or teachers' attitudes influence educational outcomes, then their influence must be shown to operate in the course of interaction among participants in actual educational environments.

Discussions of the nature of schooling rely on notions like

students' careers, school achievement, and teacher quality. These and other "educational facts" are worked out in the interaction among educators, parents, students, and others on a practical basis in everyday contexts. Because educational facts are constituted in interaction, we need to study interaction in educational contexts, both in and out of school, in order to understand the nature of schooling.

Large-scale surveys may be appropriate for studying gross differences between schools (Coleman et al., 1966; Jencks et al., 1972; Sewell, Haller, and Portes, 1969), but they are not helpful in revealing the social processes of education that take place within particular schools. By the very nature of their research design, correlational studies are unable to capture the processes of education. This limitation of large-scale surveys of schooling has been recognized by the architect of one of the most influential correlational studies in American education today (Jencks et al., 1972:13):

> We have ignored not only attitudes and values but the internal life of schools. We have been preoccupied with the effects of schooling, especially those effects that might be expected to persist into adulthood. This had led us to adopt a "factory" metaphor in which the schools are seen primarily as places that alter the characteristics of their alumini.
>
> Our research has convinced us that this is the wrong way to think about schools. The long term effects of schooling seem less significant to us now than when we began our work, and the internal life of schools seems correspondingly more important.

Karabel and Halsey (1976:531) make this point even more forcefully: "The unifying struggle for educational reform and the recrudescence of racially linked genetic theories of intelligence in the 1960's added urgency to the problem of explaining differential academic achievement. Macro sociological approaches, whatever their political and ideological correlates, have largely proven inadequate to the task."

When large-scale surveys have been the exclusive research instrument employed in educational research, very few practical policies have been produced. There are many reasons for this record (see Rosenbaum, 1976). First, correlational studies do not explain much of the data. Very little of the variance in output factors is accounted for by input (explana-tory) factors in educational research equations. Even more perplexing, when research results are cast in the form of input-output data, we have no way of knowing where to look for the missing explanatory factors. Second, correlational studies seldom provide similar findings on the same topic. There is an equivocal literature on the effects of schooling on a whole host of other factors, including economic attain-ment, social mobility, literacy, and cultural maintenance. Similarly, there is little agreement on whether ability group-ing, modifications in classroom arrangements, or bilingual instruction, among others, affects academic achievement. Third, correlational studies even produce contradictory in-terpretations of the same data. For example, Coleman et al. (1966), Jencks et al. (1972), and Bowles and Gintes (1976) all used a similar data base, yet arrived at considerably different interpretations of the influence of schooling on students' careers.

Even if correlational studies yielded unequivocal results, the nature of the data would make it difficult to draw policy implications and to implement them in actual educational settings. For one thing, data gathered and analyzed in cor-relational studies are static. Products of the educational process, such as test scores, grades, and class standing, are correlated with products of students' background experi-ence. Because the educational process itself is not a focus of study, it is not surprising that educators and policymakers have difficulty deciding which specific actions to take in order to make educational improvements. Also, the results of correlational studies are probabalistic, that is, they report average distributions across a large population of cases. As a result, educators cannot be certain that these general find-ings apply to the specific circumstances of a particular school or community. Finally, the results of correlational studies are also abstract. Presented as statistical summaries, they are far removed from the practical daily activities of educators, parents, and students. Each of the numbers in an input-output model presumably stands on behalf of a con-stellation of activities between parents with students, educators with students, and so forth; however, the activities themselves cannot be retrieved from the numerical summaries. As a result, educators have difficulty translating abstract summaries into concrete action.

In short, the tabulation of data into frequency distributions obscures the processes of interaction that take place in practical, social circumstances. Dividing the flow of interaction into discrete variables destroys the relationship of action to its practical context. The correlation of discrete variables does not reveal the interactional activity between people that produces the social structures that discrete variables presumably index.

This study is based on the premise that answers to questions about the role of schooling in society will not come from large-scale comparisons between schools, but will come from careful descriptions of what takes place inside schools. In order to understand the influence of schooling, we need research strategies that examine the living processes of education that occur within classrooms, on playgrounds, at home, and on the streets. In order to examine the processes of education that take place in these educational environments, we need to devise ways of looking at how people constitute their daily lives.

As a research strategy to serve this purpose I propose "constitutive ethnography," the description of the social organization of routine, everyday events. In educational situations, the organization of events like lessons, reading groups, task sessions, and counseling sessions is the focus of attention. A description of the interactional work of participants that assembles the structure of these events is the goal of this style of research.

In recommending constitutive ethnography as a research strategy to examine the processes of schooling, I am not claiming that this study resolves the uncertainties about the influence of schooling. My concern at this point is more to refocus attention away from the long-term effects of schooling by providing a way to search for answers in the process of educational interaction, than it is to provide a specific catalog of findings. This book, then, is as much a recommendation about how to proceed as it is a report about what will be found at the end of the journey. When this journey is completed, I believe, we will know how to look at interaction in classrooms and other educational environments to specify the interactional work that does make a difference in educational outcomes.

Research Strategies in the Study of the Classroom

This study is certainly not the first to look at interaction in an elementary school classroom. Countless researchers have crossed through schoolhouse doors seeking understanding about the educational process. However, there are significant differences between the research strategy employed in this study, constitutive ethnography, and the prevailing research strategies of the classroom, quantification schemes of classroom interaction and participant observation or field studies.

QUANTIFICATION SCHEMES OF CLASSROOM INTERAC-TION   In their review of studies of classroom interaction, Dunkin and Biddle (1974:321) made the following observation: "Most classroom observation research has focused on the frequencies of occurrences of various categories of behavior." This observation reflects the state of affairs in much of classroom research because the correlational model employed in studies of differences between schools has been, for all intents and purposes, recapitulated in studies that have taken place within schools.

Perhaps influenced by the success Bales (1950) enjoyed in quantifying aspects of small-group behavior, many schemes have developed to quantify the frequency of various patterns of classroom interaction. The Flanders system (Amidon and Flanders, 1963; Flanders, 1970) is one of the most widely used quantification schemes (see Dunkin and Biddle, 1974, for a review of many such systems). Although the exact categories used vary from scheme to scheme, the data gathering and data analysis procedures are similar in all schemes. The process involves on-the-spot coding of teacher and student behavior. Observers are provided with a set of categories and sit in a classroom and tally the action occurring around them at frequent and recurrent intervals. This technique produces a tabulation of the occurrences of certain categories of classroom behavior.

This approach to classroom observation is useful for certain purposes. However, there are serious drawbacks to an approach that limits its domain to behavior tabulated into discrete categories. The fundamental consequence is that the contingent nature of interaction is obscured. More specifically, (1) students' contributions to classroom interaction, (2) the interrelationship of verbal and nonverbal behavior, (3) the relationship of behavior to context, and (4) the functions of language are not captured when quantification schemes are employed in the classroom.

Quantification schemes are useful for tabulating aspects of classroom behavior, but because they focus almost exclusively on the teacher, they minimize the contributions of students to the organization of classroom events. The classroom is socially organized. Teachers and students work in concert to create this organization.

The traditional conception of the classroom places the teacher at the front of the room and students in neat rows of desks facing the teacher. The students' responsibility in this configuration is said to be "responding when called upon" (Dunkin and Biddle, 1974:178). This view is reinforced in a scheme like that of Flanders, which provides seven categories for "teacher talk" [(1) accepts feelings, (2) praises or encourages, (3) accepts or uses ideas of students, (4) asks questions, (5) lecturing, (6) giving directions, (7) criticizing or justifying authority], but only two for "student talk" [(8) response and (9) initiation] (for details, see Amidon and Flanders, 1963).

Let's assume for a moment that classroom life *is* a simple matter of teachers asking questions and students providing answers. A system like Flanders's that simply tabulates the number of teacher questions and student replies will still be inadequate to the task of capturing classroom interaction, because even "simple" question-answer exchanges are complex interactional productions, collaboratively assembled by teachers and students. As I will demonstrate in the following chapters, for interaction in teacher-directed lessons to proceed smoothly, questions asked by a teacher must be answered both correctly and appropriately by students. And, in order to provide an answer that is consistent with a question, the student must recognize the form of the teacher's initiation act and interpret the turn-allocation procedure in use. The initiation of action by teacher or student requires synchronization of behavior. The introduction of a topic into a lesson requires precise timing, including making turn taking coincide with a previous speaker's turn leaving.

In addition, student action in a classroom is not limited to responding when called upon. Even in teacher-directed lessons, students do more than respond to teacher-initiated acts. They greet others, provide information to the teacher and each other, give directives, evaluate others' work, comment on the course of events, and work to achieve their objectives in the context of the teacher's objectives. This wide range of student contribution is far more complex than a system like Flanders's is equipped to handle.

The situation is even more complex in student-centered classrooms, team-teaching arrangements, and learning centers. There, students often have some responsibility for organizing their course of study, deciding their length of study time, and influencing techniques of discipline. This means that students have to be particularly well attuned to demands that shift with different classroom arrangements. And in bilingual classrooms, shifting situational demands are compounded by code switching. As a result, a methodology that captures the mutual synchronization of behavior, not one that simply tabulates frequencies, is required to provide an adequate ethnography of classroom life.

Quantification schemes are useful for tabulating verbal behavior in the classroom, but because they code only talk, they do not include nonverbal contributions to the organization of classroom events. Verbal behavior and nonverbal behavior are interactionally connected in classrooms (Byers and Byers, 1972; McDermott, 1976; Erickson and Shultz, 1977), as in other naturally occurring situations (Scheflen,

1972). Students bid for the floor by raising their hands and leaning forward; teachers identify a next speaker with a head nod and hold the floor for particular students by eye contact and body orientation. A teacher can quiet a child by a touch while simultaneously asking another student a question. Body positioning, in conjunction with changes in voice pitch and rhythm, provides cues that "contextualize" behavior (Gumperz, 1971), and in so doing orients participants to what is happening in different classroom circumstances.

A description of the interconnected nature of teacher-student interaction in verbal and nonverbal modalities is required in order to capture the full range of activities that teachers and students engage in while coping with the complexities of classroom life.

Time sampling may be useful for tabulating the frequency of occurrences, but because it treats teacher and student behavior as isolated acts, it obscures the sequential flow of classroom activity. Marking tallies at regular time intervals does not reveal the contingent nature of behavior in the classroom. Student responses (Flanders's category 8) and giving praise (Flanders's category 2), for example, are not random occurrences in the classroom. They are tied together in sequences of interaction. If a teacher's action is coded as "gives praise to a student," it is important to know what that student did immediately before that action, and what other students who did not receive praise were doing. Or, if "student talks in response to teacher," did the teacher call on a student who had been seeking the teacher's attention, or did the teacher select one who had not bid for the floor? Are students who bid for the floor ignored? Are those who do not bid for the floor encouraged? There is no way to recover the sequential flow of interaction from a Flanders chart in order to answer these important questions about classroom behavior. When frequencies are merely tabulated, the overall organization of classroom events is lost.

Furthermore, tabulations based on time samplings do not show the context surrounding a tabulated entry. The social organization of the classroom can be divided into events: academic lessons, procedural meetings (such as "circles on the rug"), recess, snack time, and so on. Each of these events is guided by normative rules, and different rules apply to different events. These rules are tacit, that is, they are seldom stated in so many words. As a result, students must learn the rules that apply in each situation, be able to recognize differences between situations, and be able to produce behavior appropriate to each situation. They must know, for example, that running and shouting are acceptable during recess but not during reading, that calling out an answer is acceptable during "student's time at the rug" but not during "teacher's time at the rug" (Bremme and Erickson, 1977).

Finally, time sampled tabulations do not place the entry on a tally sheet and the event of which it is a part in the larger context of the school day, place the school day in the larger context of the school week, the school year, and so forth. The relationship of an action to these increasingly general concentric circles of context is important, for actions take on different meanings in different phases of an event, in different events, and at different times of the year.

The type of summary data produced by a quantification system like Flanders's ignores issues regarding the functions of language in the classroom (Cazden, John, and Hymes, 1972; Shuy and Griffin, 1978). A particular language function (giving a directive, making an elicitation, making a promise) can be realized by many forms of speech. For example, as Sinclair and Coulthard (1975:33) point out, a teacher could say any of the following to a student: (a) "Can you shut the door?" (b) "Would you mind shutting the door?" (c) "I wonder if you could shut the door?" (d) "The door is still open." (e) "The door . . ." Depending on their context, these utterances can take on different meanings. Utterances (a) and (c) could be either questions about a student's physical strength or directives; (d) could be either an existential statement or a directive; (e) could be either a musing or a directive.

Students need to be able to decide the meaning of these utterances by interpreting them in context. Tabulating how many times a teacher "asks a question" (Flanders's category 4) does not reveal what students need to know about language and social context in order to interpret questions and respond appropriately to them.

The simple quantification of classroom behavior also

ignores the multiple functions that any speech act can serve simultaneously. For example, a teacher can praise and elicit new information from a student in one turn of talk: "Name-cards, good. Ernesto." In a similar manner, the teacher's statement "wait a minute, raise your hand if you know the answer" both comments on past transgressions of classroom turn-allocation procedures and simultaneously instructs students how they should act to gain access to the floor. By the same token, the teacher's praise of a student's action, such as "Brad raised his hand very nicely," simultaneously instructs other students on proper procedures. Quantification schemes, by forcing observers to make discrete choices among categories and by not presenting the materials upon which coding decisions were based, fail to reflect accurately the multiple, simultaneous functions that language serves in the classroom.

In short, the quantitative approach to classroom observation is useful for certain purposes, namely, for providing the frequency of teacher talk by comparison with student talk and tabulating the frequency of certain acts of speech that can be noticed by a nonparticipant. However, this approach minimizes the contribution of students, neglects the interrelationship of verbal to nonverbal behavior, obscures the contingent nature of interaction, and ignores the (often multiple) functions of language. As a result it has limited utility for a rigorous description of the internal life of schools.

CONVENTIONAL FIELD STUDIES   Understanding the complexity of classroom life requires a more holistic approach, one that considers the classroom situation in its totality and places it in a wider social context. "Participant observation" has contributed to this holistic approach. Researchers who employ a participant observation research strategy have examined the "internal life of schools" that is left untouched by correlational studies and quantification schemes. Field researchers are generally interested in describing the systematic patterns of routine behaviors that occur in social situations. To do this they adopt some version of a participant observation role in the social situations they study. They document the activities of the participants in the scenes they describe.

The field research approach applied to the school is characterized by detailed descriptions of a small number of school events. Unlike the survey, the purpose of the field study is more to describe what has happened than to provide a correlational analysis. Descriptions of schooling in other societies (Redfield, 1943; Wylie, 1957; Warren, 1967), studies of routine classroom events in this society (Jackson, 1968; Smith and Geoffrey, 1968; Rist, 1970), chronicles of days in the life of school participants (Wolcott, 1973), and natural histories of school activities (Burnett, 1969), have employed the field research approach.

Field studies have a number of positive features. Often when I complete reading a report of field research, I have a sense of presence; I feel as if I have been there. Furnished with rich details about the setting, I can often smell the smells and hear the noise. I find myself nodding my head in affirmation of the descriptions. Participant observers often live through traumatic experiences in the field. Many researchers convey these experiences in passionate prose in the pages of their reports.

Field studies of the school, however, also have a number of difficulties. As is so often the case, the strengths of an enterprise are also its weaknesses. First, conventional field reports tend to have an antecdotal quality. Research reports include a few exemplary instances of the behavior that the researcher has culled from field notes. Second, these researchers seldom provide their criteria or grounds for including certain instances and not others. As a result, it is difficult to determine the typicality and representativeness of instances and findings generated from them. Third, research reports presented in tabular or summary form do not preserve the materials upon which the analysis was conducted. As the researcher abstracts data from raw materials to produce summarized findings, the original form of the materials is lost. Therefore, it is impossible to entertain alternative interpretations of the same materials.

Audiovisual equipment has been employed as a data gathering device in order to overcome some of these shortcomings in conventional field studies (Cicourel et al., 1974). Videotape and film are helpful in field research because they preserve research materials in close to their original form. Videotape and film also serve as an extrasomatic "memory" that allows researchers to examine materials extensively and repeatedly. Furthermore, basic materials can be presented along with an analysis to document conclusions and to allow alternative interpretations.

Unfortunately, audiovisual materials, in and of themselves, do not overcome the lack of rigor in conventional field studies. Because of the richness of audiovisual materials, many researchers collect one or two short segments of interaction and analyze them in great detail. However, this practice makes it impossible to determine the relationship of these isolated segments to the context from which they were taken. It also makes it difficult to determine the frequency or typicality of their occurrence. As a result, research reports based on audiovisual materials still tend to have an ad hoc quality (Cicourel et al., 1974). Instead of presenting tidbits of data obtained from field notes, researchers have presented tidbits of audiovisual materials or transcripts. Although audiovisual equipment enables materials to be preserved, recovered, and presented to audiences, exhaustive analysis of classroom activities has not been achieved in conventional field studies of the school.

For these reasons, a number of researchers have both modified the conventional field research strategy and changed the phenomena of research interest in the study of educational settings. While conventional field studies are conducted to describe the systematic patterns of routine social behavior, "constitutive ethnographies" are conducted to describe the interactional work that assembles those systematic patterns.

CONSTITUTIVE ETHNOGRAPHY   Correlational studies, the prevailing research strategy in the study of the school, are conducted to measure associations between structural or cognitive variables. While correlational studies provide aggregate data about the relations between input and output factors, they shed little light on the processes of education.

Field studies have provided descriptions of some of the recurrent patterns of behavior occurring in schools that are not captured by correlational studies. However, these descriptions have not been very systematic. Field research reports do not include the rules by which data are abstracted from observed materials. As·a result, field studies give us no way to figure out what makes a difference in educational outcomes.

In seeking correlations or simply describing recurrent patterns of behavior, educational researchers of the two most common methodological persuasions (field studies and correlational studies) have ignored the very ways in which these "objective and constraining social facts" of the educational world come about. A third research perspective, which has only recently been applied to education, seeks to counter this omission by studying the "social structuring activities" that assemble social structures in educational settings.

A number of different names have been applied to this perspective. McDermott (1976), perhaps influenced by Scheflen (1972), at one point refers to his work as "context analysis." Erickson and his associates at the Harvard Graduate School of Education refer to their work as "microethnography" (see Erickson and Shultz, 1978; Erickson, 1975; Shultz, 1976; Bremme and Erickson, 1977; Florio, 1978). I prefer the term "constitutive ethnography" to "microethnography" for two reasons. First, the term microethnography can unwittingly perpetuate the unfortunate macro-micro distinction in sociology by suggesting that only minutia are under study while "larger social structures" are being ignored. The origins of this problem are visible in early ethnomethodology. Early ethnomethodologists argued that sociologists, in their search for regularities in social structures, ignored the structuring activities that result in these structures. In so arguing, early ethnomethodologists swung the pendulum of social theory from an exclusive concern for social facts to an equally exclusive concern for members' methods, accounting practices, constitutive presuppositions, and the like. Constitutive

ethnography in school settings is overcoming this constitutive bias (Mehan and Wood, 1975:194-197) by not treating
structuring separately from structures. Constitutive ethnographies of schooling neither deny the facticity of the social
world nor give priority to structuring activities over social
structures. Constitutive studies put structure and structuring
on an equal footing by showing *how* the social facts of the
world emerge from structuring work to become external and
constraining, as part of a world that is at once of our making
and beyond our making (Mehan and Wood, 1975:201-203).

Second, Smith and Geoffrey (1968) have already adopted
the term microethnography to characterize what I describe
here as a participant observation study, that is, a description
of recurrent patterns of behavior in a school context, without
an accompanying concern for the interactional "work" that
generates these discovered patterns. Since, in fact, a concern of this third research perspective is to make linkages between macro and micro by showing the construction of
structure at many levels of analysis, I have adopted the term
constitutive ethnography in order to avoid these unintended
consequences.

Constitutive studies operate on the premise that social
structures are interactional accomplishments (Garfinkel,
1967; Garfinkel and Sacks, 1970; Cicourel, 1968; Scheflen,
1972). The central recommendation of constitutive studies of
the school is that "objective social facts" like students' intelligence, academic achievement, or career paths and "routine
patterns of behavior" like classroom organizational arrangements are accomplished in the interaction between teachers
and students, testers and students, principals and teachers,
and so on. Therefore, constitutive ethnographers study the
structuring activities and the social facts of education they
constitute rather than merely describing recurrent patterns or
seeking correlations among antecedent and consequent
variables.

In addition to this theoretical interest in social structures
and social structuring, there are methodological policies that
distinguish constitutive studies from other research strategies

used in the school. The constitutive analysis of the structuring of school structure aims for (1) retrievability of data, (2) comprehensive data treatment, (3) a convergence between researchers' and participants' perspectives on events, and (4) an interactional level of analysis.

Retrievability of data. Conventional research reports do not usually preserve or present the materials upon which an analysis was conducted. Research findings are presented in tabulated or summary form to corroborate orienting hypotheses. As the researcher moves up the ladder of abstraction from raw materials through coded data to summarized findings, the materials are not retained in anything that resembles their original form. As a result, the opportunity to consider alternative interpretations of the same material is lost.

Constitutive studies employ videotape and film as data gathering and data display devices. Audiovisual materials are used in this way because they preserve data in close to their original form. Videotape serves as an external memory that allows researchers to examine materials extensively and repeatedly, often frame-by-frame in the case of 16 mm film (Erickson and Shultz, 1978; McDermott, 1976).

In some constitutive studies, as in this one, audio portions of videotape are transcribed. Utterances are attributed to speakers, numbered for ease of reference, and sequentially arranged. Some researchers, especially those influenced by Scheflen (1972) (for example, Erickson and Shultz, 1978; Shultz, 1976; McDermott, 1976; McDermott and Aron, in press) have incorporated nonverbal behavior into the analysis.

Constitutive studies often include transcripts and videotape along with reports of analyses as the grounds of their interpretations (see Mehan et al., 1976; Cicourel et al., 1974). It is recognized that the videotape is not the phenomenon per se, but is a theoretically motivated perspectival view. In effect, constitutive analysts are conducting an "ethnography of ethnography" (Berreman, 1972), that is, a method that preserves materials so that they can be retrieved as they are transformed into data and analyzed (Cicourel, 1968:2; Mehan, 1973:328) and a method of documenting sources and the basis of inferences.

Comprehensive data treatment.   Researchers must be on guard against the tendency to seek only that evidence which supports their orienting hypotheses or domain assumptions (Campbell and Fiske, 1959). When research reports include only a few exemplary instances that support a researcher's claims, it is difficult to entertain alternative interpretations of the data.

A policy guiding constitutive ethnography is a comprehensive analysis of the entire corpus of materials. In this particular study, the goal is to construct a model that accounts for the organization of each and every instance of teacher-student interaction in the nine lessons in the corpus.

This policy represents a departure from the ordinary statistical way of studying social relations with correlations, which Robinson (1951) has termed "enumerative induction." Correlational analysis typically seeks cases in which instances of two or more phenomena co-occur. If such researchers are doing their work thoroughly, they also look for cases in which instances of the phenomena do not occur together. The logic of this procedure is illustrated in figure 1.1, where A and B represent the positive occurrence of phenomena (cell 1), and $\overline{A}$ and $\overline{B}$ represent nonoccurrences of the phenomena (cell 4).

FIGURE 1.1. CO-OCCURRENCE RELATIONSHIPS
BETWEEN TWO PHENOMENA.

	A	$\overline{A}$
B	AB cell 1	$\overline{A}$B cell 2
$\overline{B}$	A$\overline{B}$ cell 3	$\overline{AB}$ cell 4

Although cases remain in cells 2 and 3, investigators using enumerative induction usually do not push their analysis until they have a complete explanation of all cases. If statistically significant correlations are obtained even when data appear in cells 2 and 3, investigators using enumerative induction are content to leave relatively low frequencies in these cells unexplained (Robinson, 1951). The policy guiding constitutive research demands that all cases of data be incorporated in the analysis. This policy is adopted because people in social situations are making sense all the time. Since this is the case, anomalies cannot be left unanalyzed, for participants are acting in some purposeful way even at these "anomalous" times. In order to assemble a complete description of social interaction, the researcher must account for the organization of participants' sense making at all times.

This comprehensive data analysis is accomplished by a method that is analogous to "analytic induction" (Znaniecki, 1934:232-233; Robinson, 1951). The method begins with a small batch of data. A provisional analytic scheme is generated. The scheme is then compared to other data, and modifications are made in the scheme as necessary. The provisional analytic scheme is constantly confronted by "negative" or "discrepant" cases until the researcher has derived a small set of recursive rules that incorporate all the data in the corpus. The result is an integrated, precise model that comprehensively describes a specific phenomena, instead of a simple correlational statement about antecedent and consequent conditions.

This approach should not be confused with "deviant case analysis" as that term has been employed in the analysis of survey data (Lazarsfeld and Rosenberg, 1964:111-114). The survey researcher analyzes deviant cases when the available explanatory variables have been exhausted, but explanatory closure has not been reached because residual cases remain. At such times, the survey researcher looks for new variables to correlate with the residuals, resulting in a "multivariate analysis" (Lazarsfeld and Rosenberg, 1964:112). In the chapters that follow, when some but not all of the data have been accounted for by the provisional analytic scheme, new variables are not added. Instead, the analytic scheme is modified until all the data are accounted for.

The social organization of all teacher-student interaction in the corpus of materials studied here is described in this manner. Transcripts and videotapes are analyzed and form the data base for discussions of classroom interaction. When instances of these materials are included in the text accompanying the analysis, they represent classes of data that have been analyzed comprehensively. These practices help insure that confirming evidence, as well as the absence of disconfirming evidence, is documented.

Convergence between researchers' and participants' perspectives. A constitutive ethnography seeks to insure that the structure and structuring of events described by the researcher converges with that of the participants in the event. That is, the phenomenon that the researcher locates upon analysis must also be a phenomenon that orients participants (compare Garfinkel and Sacks, 1970:345; Mehan and Wood, 1975:181).

One way in which the "psychological reality" of ethnographic findings has been tested has been by "elicitation frames." After ethnographers have constructed a candidate version of some aspect of the group's culture, such as genealogical taxonomies, they ask group members questions about the phenomenon. If the group members' answers to the elicitation questions match the ethnographer's analysis, then ethnographers can have some confidence in the validity of their findings (see, for example, Tyler, 1969).

However, as Frake (1977) reminds us, "plying frames can be dangerous," because the very act of eliciting information structures the respondents' answers (compare Cicourel, 1964, 1975; Mehan and Wood, 1975:13-14, 54-60). Far from providing independent verification, information from elicitation frames provides convergent validation (Campbell and Fiske, 1959) of the findings.

The test of members' recognition cannot be passed, therefore, by polling, naming, or other use of elicitation devices. In this study, I turn to participants' naturally occurring behavior rather than elicitation frames or other polling techniques to insure that the machinery of the lessons described actually orients the behavior of the participants during the course of their interaction.

More specifically, in order to determine whether or not a phenomenon uncovered by a researcher is also a participant's phenomenon, I consider the consequences of action in the course of the event. If a researcher's description of the organization of an event is valid, the participants within that event will orient to its structural features during the course of their interaction (compare McDermott, 1976:153-158; McDermott, Gospodinoff, and Aron, 1978). They will make the researcher's phenomenon visible by their actions, especially in the absence of expected forms of interaction.

The classroom participants in this study mark the sequential organization of classroom lessons by verbal, paralinguistic, and kinesic means (see chapters 2 and 3). They make classroom rules visible by accounting for the absence of expected occurrences and by sanctioning violations (see chapter 3; compare McDermott, 1976:158-161; McDermott, Gospodinoff, and Aron, 1978). Participants' orientation to the organization of lessons, including accounting for the absence of expected forms of interaction, helps make the normally unnoticed structure of lessons visible.

Interactional level of analysis. Since classroom events are socially organized, a constitutive analysis has the further commitment to locate this organization in the interaction itself (compare McDermott, 1976:144-149; McDermott, Gospodinoff, and Aron, 1978). The analysis starts with a particular aspect of the event and continues until a small set of recursive coding rules is located that completely describes the organization of the event.

The behavior displayed in the interaction between participants is the primary source of data. The goal is to locate the organizing machinery of classroom lessons in the interaction, as a "cohort's practical, situated accomplishment" (Garfinkel and Sacks, 1970:346; compare Mehan and Wood, 1975:81-82). Since the organization is accomplished by participants' interactional work in the web of practical class-room circumstances, evidence for the organizational machinery of lessons is to be found in the words and in the gestures of the participants. The policy "If it is a phenomenon, it must be in the interaction" (Sacks, 1963) establishes a strong methodological maxim. Unfounded attributions to the mental states or intentions of the participants, unwarranted psychological reduction, and the reification of unobservable, abstracted sociological notions can be avoided by conforming to this policy.

The Conduct of the Inquiry

A number of theoretical concerns and practical circumstances influenced the way in which this particular study was conducted. These interests and circumstances coincided to produce the nine lessons that serve as the corpus of materials for the study.

THE SETTING The school that served as the setting for this study is in a black and Mexican-American neighborhood in Southeast San Diego. A large shopping center, a number of fundamentalist churches, a laundry business, and small frame houses dot the perimeter of the school. Many students must cross a busy highway (which eliminated some homes when it was built) to get to school.

The two hundred or so families that send their children to this school have demographic features that are characteristic of the inner city: 52 percent are below the poverty line; 25 percent of the heads of household are unemployed; 67 percent of the employed are in semiskilled or unskilled occupations; 33 percent of the heads of household are female; 55 percent have less than a high school education; and 50 percent of the families have more than five members.

The neighborhood around the school is in transition. Like other inner-city neighborhoods, its overall population is shrinking. A decade ago, the neighborhood was inhabited primarily by blacks. As blacks moved from Southeast San Diego to East San Diego to buy single-family homes, they were replaced by Mexican-Americans, moving north from the border to seek employment in skilled and semiskilled jobs.

This changing ethnic composition is reflected in the population of the school. While the upper grades are approximately 60 percent black, 35 percent Mexican-American, this ratio is equalized in the lower grades. The combined first, second, and third grade classroom studied reflected the new ethnic mix of the school and the neighborhood, having equal numbers of Mexican-Americans and blacks.

DATA GATHERING   Figure 1.2 is a diagram of the classroom as it was arranged in the fall during the time of this study. Either one of my research associates (Fisher, Maroules) or I observed in the classroom on a regular basis in order to get an overall sense of classroom activities and to decide on a videotaping schedule.

FIGURE 1.2. ROOM 24 IN FALL OF YEAR.

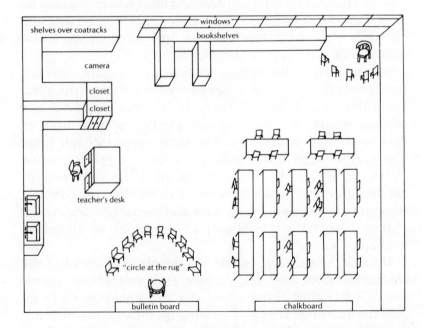

We videotaped the first hour of school activities every day of the first week of school, and one hour a day approximately every third week until April. At that time we changed our research focus from teacher-student to student-student interaction. These results are being analyzed separately. For interim reports, see Cazden (1977), Cazden et al. (1978), and Mehan (1977a, 1977b).

This schedule was influenced by a combination of practical circumstances and theoretical interests. The one-hour unit of analysis was selected because videotape for the portable studio equipment we had available was one hour long. The first hour of the day was chosen because of our theoretical interest in the skills and abilities that students must use in order to be competent members of the classroom community. This interest suggested that we study teacher-student interaction in both formal and informal classroom activities. The first hour of the day promised to have the best mix of academic and procedural activities. The day began with students being served snacks and informally interacting at their desks. Then the students were gathered together on the rug to hear the schedule for the day, join in "show and tell," and receive informal instruction. The first hour was concluded by more formal instruction. The teacher either worked with the class as a whole or divided the class into small groups for instruction in math and language arts.

We videotaped the first hour of the day at regular intervals throughout the school year because of our theoretical interest in the socialization of students into the academic and normative demands of the classroom. We have a corpus of data, with nine instances of the same event through time. This corpus helps insure that our analysis depicts routine classroom events, thereby strengthening the generality of our findings. It also enables us to determine whether the structure of classroom interaction and students' competence change through the school year. (These issues are addressed in chapter 4.)

The daily schedule of events and the physical layout of the classroom influenced our camera and microphone placement. The clothes closet afforded a convenient place to locate the videorecorder and viewing monitor. Once the students placed sweaters and lunches in this corner at the start of the day, it was relatively unoccupied for the remainder of the day. High shelves blocked sound and sight from the rest of the room. As the closet was in a corner, a wide diagonal view of the room was available.

Two microphones were placed in the ceiling over the major instructional centers—one near the rug area and one near the blackboard from which the teacher taught math and reading. We switched microphones as instructional activity moved from one part of the room to the other.

A combination of practical circumstances and theoretical concerns reduced our corpus of materials from thirteen hours of classroom activity to nine "classroom lessons." The most notable practical constraint was sound quality. The microphones placed in the ceiling over the two major instructional centers were adequate to capture conversation in the dominant teacher-centered channel of communication. However, they were not adequate to record student voices when students were not directly involved with the teacher. As a result, we were forced to concentrate our analysis on classroom events with the teacher as the locus of activity.

We settled on the name "lessons" for these activities. This selection of terms was informed by the participants themselves. Members of a community often formulate the name of an event (that is, name it in so many words) as a natural part of their interaction (Frake, 1964, 1977; McDermott, 1976), or can provide the name in response to an explicit question like "what's going on here?" (Agar, 1975). We would often ask the teacher, "What are you going to do today?" She would answer with formulations like "have a circle on the rug," "conduct math lessons," or "conduct reading lessons." The teacher also annotated her daily and weekly schedules with such terms. Finally, we heard the teacher (and later the students) use the name "lessons" as they assembled at certain parts of the room at certain times of the day.

At the outset of an analysis, events can be glossed as the names given to activities by their participants. But the analysis cannot stop there. A goal of constitutive ethnography is to describe the social organization of events in such a way that is acceptable to participants. That means starting with members' explicit formulations, then analyzing the materials until the interactional "work" of participants that accomplishes the social organization of the event that they originally formulated is located.

DATA ANALYSIS The next step of the inquiry, and the first step of the analysis, involved the interior of lessons. The orienting concern was to see what teachers and students did to accomplish the social organization of the event that participants and researchers originally formulated as lessons.

Videotapes of lessons from the first week of school served as a first, exploratory, panel of data. These tapes were viewed repeatedly, and the audio portion of the videotape was rerecorded using a Uher 5000. Transcriptions of the audio portion were made in the conventional way (see Mehan, 1974a:131-142) for an example of this preliminary transcription form). This transcript was then checked against the videotape. Information about speakers' identities, some talk, and nonverbal behavior that was not available in the rerecording of the audio portion of the videotape were added to the transcript.

Analysis of the first panel of data located the basic initiation-reply-evaluation sequences described in chapter 2 and the basic turn-allocation procedures described in chapter 3. This provisional analytic scheme based on the first panel of data was then tested against panels of data gathered later in the fall and winter. Analysis of these panels of data required a modification of the initial model. Notably, extended sequences, topically related sets of sequences, the hierarchical structure of lessons, and the recurrent verbal, paralinguistic, and kinesic "markers" were discovered upon analysis of these later tapes (see chapter 2). The improvisational strategies and students' initiatory activities also became apparent in this subsequent analysis (see chapters 3 and 4). This additional analytic machinery, derived from the analysis of the second and third panels of data, was then reapplied to the first panel of data and incorporated into the final model of the social organization of classroom lessons.

This approach is similar to the methods employed by Erickson's group (Erickson and Shultz, 1977; Florio, 1978; Shultz,

1976; Erickson, 1975), McDermott and his associates (McDermott, 1976; McDermott and Aron, 1977; McDermott, Gospodinoff, and Aron, 1978; McDermott and Church, 1977), and Shuy and Griffin (1978) in their related analyses of classroom interaction. It should also be compared to the method Brown used in his psycholinguistic analysis of language acquisition (1973). Each of these analyses starts with a small batch of data and examines increasing amounts of context surrounding the data until a comprehensive description is obtained.

CODING AS A HEURISTIC DEVICE An observation about the status of the coding scheme is in order at this point. Classroom interaction, like other forms of interaction, has a unitary character; its seams are tightly woven.

The purpose of analysis is to make the unitary discrete by exposing its seams and dividing the whole into parts. This act of analysis, when applied to our classroom materials, requires the assignment of status of "utterance," "interactional sequence," "turn-taking procedure," and the like, to portions of the interactional flow. As talk and gestures are coded as instances of categories, the integrity of this flow is disturbed. The very act of coding requires that materials be treated as conforming to the law of the excluded middle, that is, each instance can be placed in only one category at a time.

This coding activity is not an end in itself, but a means to an end. We recognize at the outset that the boundaries between events are not discrete, that speech acts perform multiple tasks simultaneously, that the meaning of an action is not necessarily shared among participants or between participants and observers.

We code our materials into discrete categories because we do not want to be overwhelmed by the very flux that we are trying to comprehend. Interaction is too massive to be addressed in its entirety all at once. Our structural analysis facilitates a closer examination of representative instances of certain categories or all instances of particularly interesting categories.

Thus, our coding scheme is heuristic device employed to

stop the action portrayed in the videotape while attempting to remain faithful to the flow of interaction.

THE CORPUS OF MATERIALS   The following is a summary of the nine lessons in our corpus. The complete transcripts of these lessons appear in Mehan et al., 1976.

CIS #3: S and M Words.   This reading preparedness lesson was conducted on September 18, 1974, which was the third day of school. The teacher was at the chalkboard. The students were in their seats facing her.

In this lesson, the teacher wanted students to identify words that start with the letter *S* and the letter *M*. At the outset of the lesson, the teacher put a chart on the chalkboard. She asked students to identify the letter *S* and the letter *M*, provide names that start with *S*, names that start with *M*, and names of foods that start with those letters. After a list was assembled and entered on the chart, she asked the students to repeat all the words they had identified.

CIS #4: Namecards.   This lesson was conducted on September 19, 1974, the fourth day of the first week of school. It combined elements of reading and sociability. The teacher was checking to see who could read while having students get to know each other better.

The students were assembled in a circle around the teacher in the rug area. The teacher had a pile of cards in her lap, each of which had the name of a student on it. She held up a namecard and engaged the students in a series of questions concerning it. She asked students to identify the card, and often to locate that student in the room. If she had students link the name to a student, then she asked that student to confirm the identification.

CIS #4: The Map.   This lesson occurred immediately after the Namecards lesson at the circle on the fourth day. This lesson was a continuation of the teacher's use of a large-scale representation of the schoolyard mounted on the wall behind the group. The day before, the teacher and students had explored the schoolyard and had drawn pictures of objects they had located on their walk. In this lesson the teacher continued locating objects on the map, including the road grader, a nearby street, and a student's house.

CIS #4: S and J Words. This lesson occurred immediately after the Map lesson. The teacher moved the students from the circle area back to their seats. She drew a chart similar to the one in the *S* and *M* lesson from the day before on the board. She then elicited words that start with *J* and asked students to match words starting with *S* and *J* that she provided.

CIS #4: Whistle for Willy. This interlude occurred after the *S* and *J* Words lesson and before the "seat work" for the rest of the morning on the fourth day. The teacher was at the chalkboard. She had equipped the record player with six headsets. She determined who had already listened to the "Whistle for Willy" story, obtained volunteers, and then determined how many more students could listen before she began reading-group activities.

CIS #5: Map Words. This reading lesson was conducted on September 20, 1974, the fifth day of school, at the circle, on the rug. Its topic developed from the earlier activity of constructing a map of the schoolyard. The teacher wrote a story about the map of the schoolyard and mounted it on a storyboard. The story read:

The Map

This is a map.
See Room 24.
See the machine.
See the street.
See the cafeteria.
We eat in the cafeteria.

The lesson had two parts. In the first part, the teacher elicited recitations of the title and lines of the story from the students. In the second part of the lesson, the teacher placed three-by-five cards with words from the story on the floor in front of the students. They were instructed to choose a card and match it to an equivalent word on the storyboard.

CIS #7: Cafeteria Trays. This lesson took place on November 7, 1974, while the teacher was at the blackboard and the students were in their seats. The lesson concerned developing an improved cafeteria procedure. The teacher presented the students with three alternatives for returning their cafeteria trays after lunch: (1) teacher to return trays, (2) each child to return a tray, (3) designated "tray helpers" to return trays.

In the first part of the lesson, the teacher had students describe the alternative they preferred and explain their choice. In the second part of the lesson, the students voted on the procedure and tallied the votes.

CIS #8: Birthplaces. As the school year progressed, the teacher extended the map conception from the school yard to the local neighborhood and, finally, to the United States and Mexico. On November 18, 1974, the teacher asked the students to bring information from home about family members' birthplaces. The students brought pieces of paper explaining where their mothers, fathers, sisters, and brothers had been born. The teacher assembled the students in a circle around a large map of the United States and Mexico hung on the wall. She asked students about their own birthplaces and then about the birthplaces of members of their families. The teacher then placed pins of different colors on the map showing where the various people had been born.

CIS #9: A Martin Luther King Story. The teacher used the occasion of the anniversary of Martin Luther King's birthday (January 16, 1975) to read a story about King's childhood to the students while they were assembled in a circle on the rug. During the course of reading the book, questions about various people's ages relative to King's assassination came up in conversation.

OVERVIEW The methodological goal of this constitutive ethnography is to describe the organization of teacher-student interaction in the nine lessons from this classroom in accordance with the policies outlined above. To do so, the data were analyzed until a small set of recursive rules was located in the interaction that describes the corpus of materials in their entirety, and in terms that are oriented to by the participants themselves. The application of this strategy produces an adequate description of the organization of classroom lessons and the participants' interactional work that accomplishes that organization.

The structure of classroom lessons, including sequential and hierarchical arrangements, is described in chapter 2. The structuring of these lessons, that is, the interactional activities of the participants that assemble the lessons' organized character, is described in chapter 3. Included there are the basic procedures and improvisational strategies that are employed for this purpose.

This aspect of the analysis is important both for a theory of interaction and for an understanding of teaching and learning. For a theory of interaction, knowledge about the structure of classroom lessons will be instructive for understanding the negotiation of meaning, the use of language, and the construction of behavior in a social context. But there is educational significance in this aspect of the investigation, which, after all, is situated in an elementary school. The choice of a school as a research setting is not fortuitous; that choice is motivated by the conviction that understanding the process of interaction has practical consequences for education. The phenomenon being described is the classroom lesson, one of the most ubiquitous events in the school. A systematic description of what goes on in lessons will tell us about how the process of learning unfolds in naturally occurring school situations, knowledge that, in turn, will inform us about the influence of schooling.

In chapter 4, some of the skills involved in competent membership in the classroom community are analyzed. I point out there that learning lessons involves presenting correct academic information in interactionally appropriate ways.

This aspect of the analysis is important, in general, because it contributes to a theory of competence, and it is important, in particular, because it sheds light on the skills and abilities that students need to display in order to be considered successful in an important classroom endeavor. "Success" in educational settings has often been gauged entirely in terms of academic knowledge, while social behavior has been assigned residual status. I will show that participation in classroom lessons involves the integration of academic knowledge and social or interactional skills. This finding recommends a modification of the prevailing conception of membership in the classroom community.

This aspect of the analysis also addresses the relationship of socialization to education in formal schooling. Certainly, students are learning academic material as the school year progresses. But since we find interactional competence to be a necessary companion to academic knowledge in classroom participation, it is important to know whether students give evidence of learning the skills necessary for interaction through time as well.

In the fifth and final chapter, the nature of findings from constitutive ethnography, the relationship of the constitutive approach to previous studies of classroom interaction, differences between the organization of talking in classrooms and in everyday life situations, and new directions for this style of work are placed in the context of some more general issues.

For the reader interested in more detail, this analysis can be supplemented by the corpus of materials upon which the analysis is based. The complete set of transcripts of the nine lessons discussed in the following chapters appears elsewhere (Mehan et al., 1976). These transcripts have been coded according to the instructional function of the interactional sequences within the lessons, and according to the turn-allocation procedures employed in these lessons. A description of the codes used for these purposes appears in Part I, and rosters of important aspects of lessons appear in Part II, of Mehan et al. (1976). Included there are ways to locate all types of interactional sequences and topically related sets referred to in chapter 2, and the turn-allocation procedures described in chapter 3.

2 THE STRUCTURE OF CLASSROOM LESSONS

AS STATED IN chapter 1, the goal of this constitutive ethnography is to characterize the organization of teacher-student interaction in classroom lessons. This project involves describing the structure of these lessons and the interactional work of the participants that assembles that structure. The policies of a constitutive ethnography require that three criteria be met: first, the organization described by the researcher must, in fact, be the organization employed by the participants; second, the analysis must be retrievable from the materials; and third, the analysis must be comprehensive.

I describe classroom lessons as having a sequential organization and a hierarchical organization. Sequential organization refers to the flow of the lesson as it unfolds through time from beginning to end. Hierarchical organization refers to the assembly of the lesson into its component parts.

The analysis in this chapter will show that the participants demonstrate their orientation toward each sequential and hierarchical component of the lessons. Transcripts from videotape of each of the lessons and instructions for locating complete data classes are presented along with the analysis. This procedure enables the grounds of the interpretations to be retrieved from the materials of the study.

The Organization of Classroom Lessons

The social organization of lessons begins well before their formal opening. The teacher and students engage in recurrent interactional activity that serves to mark off the lesson from other classroom events. Like other classroom events (Erickson and Shultz, 1977; Florio, 1978; McDermott, 1976; Shultz, 1976), once a lesson is "set up," it is organized sequentially into component parts: an opening phase, an instructional phase, and a closing phase. In the opening phase, the teacher and students inform each other that they are, in fact, going to conduct a lesson as opposed to some other activity. The instructional phase is the heart of the lesson. It is during this phase that academic information is exchanged between teachers and students. In the final, closing phase, the teacher and students formulate what they have done and prepare to move on to other classroom activities.

The work or organizing, conducting, and closing lessons is accomplished by and revealed in the verbal and nonverbal behavior of lesson participants. More specifically, teacher and student behavior is organized into "interactional sequences," which perform distinctive functions in specific places in the organization of lessons. Directive and informative sequences contribute to the assembly of opening and closing phases, while the instructional phase is composed primarily of elicitation sequences.[1]

SETTING UP A LESSON The totality of activity that classroom participants and researchers alike come to call a "lesson" is set apart from other classroom activity in a number of ways. Prior to the actual lesson itself, the teacher assembled students in one of two places in the room, either at their desks or at the rug (see figure 1.2). If a lesson was to occur at the rug, the teacher directed the students to arrange their chairs in a circle facing her chair, which was positioned in front of the bulletin board (as in the Namecards, Birthplaces, Martin Luther King, and Map lessons). If a lesson was to occur at the chalkboard, the teacher either returned the students to their seats from other parts of the room (as in the S and M Words and S and J Words lessons) or if they were already in their chairs, directed their attention away from other instructional materials and activities and toward the chalkboard (as in the Whistle for Willy and Cafeteria Trays lessons).

Once the participants were assembled in one of these two instructional centers, they informed each other that they were about to participate in a lesson. On some occasions, the teacher stood in front of the chalkboard, oriented toward the students, who were seated at their desks facing toward the board. These orientations contrasted with those of other activities that took place while the students were at their desks. When students worked with materials at their desks, the teacher moved around the room assisting individual students. When the lesson took place at the rug, the teacher shifted from a standing to a sitting position and sat in a chair facing the students who were in a semicircle facing her. These wholesale physical rearrangements (changing the location of the group in the room) and these large-scale shifts in posture (the teacher moving to the chalkboard to face students while they cleared their desks and faced the board, or assembling a circle in chairs at the rug) are unique. They occur only at the beginning of the activity called a lesson, and at no other time. This unique configuration of proxemic shifts both serves to mark lessons off from other classroom activities and informs the students that that particular classroom activity, and not some other, is to begin.

OPENING THE LESSON   After the group has been physically assembled at one of the two instructional centers, the participants begin the lesson. Two kinds of activities are accomplished during this phase of the lesson: information is provided about what is going to happen during the main course of the lesson, and participants are physically rearranged to prepare for instruction.

The beginning of the S and M Words lesson displays these two activities:[2]

Initiation	Reply	Evaluation
3:1		
T: These four people over to Martin.	Many: (move to seats)	T: Good, Rafael.

Initiation	Reply	Evaluation
3:2 T: Now these four people.	Many: (move to seats)	T: Good.
3:3 T: Ok, this is some work for the people in these rows of chairs (gestures first rows).	Many: (nod heads)	T: Good.
3:4 T: Alberto, turn around so you can see the blackboard.	A: (turns; teacher assists)	

The first two lines of this transcript (3:1-3:2) represent the setup phase of the lesson described in the previous section. With the group assembled, the teacher informed the participants about the work to be done (3:3) and directed Alberto's attention to the center of instruction (3:4).

Sometimes the formulation of what is to happen takes the form of an extended soliloquy by the teacher, as at the beginning of the Cafeteria Trays lesson:

Initiation	Reply	Evaluation
7:1 T: Um, now, uh, let me ask you about something about lunch. You people have been doing a very good job as I said, yesterday, about walking to the cafeteria and back without cutting.		

Initiation	Reply	Evaluation
	Prenda: Uh, huh, and . . .	
	Others: Yes.	
7:2 T: That part's been ok, right, Prenda.	Prenda: Yeah.	
7:3 T: We're still not so good about coming back into the room. Um, but the, but the cutting isn't, the no cutting is really worked well.		
7:4 T: Now let me ask you something about in the cafeteria. Somebody has to take your trays and empty them, and put them //	//Jeannie: (raises hand)	T: Wait a minute, let me finish, let me ask the question.
	Jeannie: (lowers hand)	
7:5 T: Now, there are several different ways we can do that (writes on board): Ms. C. can empty trays (continues to write) . . .	__: Mrs. C?	

Initiation	Reply	Evaluation
Uh, each child can empty his or her own tray, or we could have tray helpers um (continues writing on board) . . . that had a job for a day of getting up and take, helping me, ah, empty the trays.	Jeannie: (raises and lowers hand)	

While the students' responses to these introductory remarks can be characterized as "acknowledgment" (Sinclair and Coulthard, 1975), this does not mean that the students are simply passive. The transcripts and the videotape from which the transcripts are derived show that the successful accomplishment of these interactional sequences requires active listening on the part of the students. They are making eye contact with the teacher, nodding their heads, and providing comments ("yeah"). The presence of such "back channel" work (Duncan, 1972) even during a seemingly passive activity like acknowledging or receiving information demonstrates that the assembly of classroom events is a joint accomplishment of teachers and students.

The students' active contribution to the formulation of what is happening is displayed at the outset of the Name-cards lesson. As the teacher sorted cards with children's names on them in her lap, the following exchanges took place:

Initiation	Reply	Evaluation
4:1 T: (shuffles cards on lap) Okay.		

Initiation	Reply	Evaluation

4:2
  C: Namecards.
		T: Namecards, right
		    Carolyn.

4:3
  T: Um, let's see, uh,
    Sabrina and
    Carolyn, sit down,
    uh, on the floor so
    everyone can, so
    you can see.
	C & S: (raise hands)	

The teacher praised Carolyn's identification of the cards (4:2) and then directed Carolyn and Sabrina to assume a more advantageous sitting position.

CONDUCTING THE LESSON   Once these lessons were underway, the primary activity was the exchange of academic information. The teacher and students exchanged factual information, opinions, interpretations of academic materials, and the grounds of their reasoning.

Lessons have often been characterized as sequences of questions and answers, questions asked by the teacher, answers provided by the students (Brophy and Good, 1974; Dunkin and Biddle, 1974; Mehan, 1974a; Mishler, 1975a, 1975b). A question, in turn, is generally thought of as containing a *wh* word (what, which, who, when), having subject-verb order reversed, and being spoken with rising intonation at the end of the sentence.

The definition of items on grammatical grounds has been helpful in analyzing sentences (Chomsky, 1965). However, this practice is not heuristic in the study of interactional events because the function of an utterance is not isomorphic with the form it takes in naturally occurring discourse (Gumperz and Hymes, 1964). A teacher can say to a student "The door is still open." Grammatically, that is a statement.

However, it can also function in classroom discourse as an indirect command to close the door. Likewise, the propositional content of "We don't sit on tables" is informative; but spoken in the context of a student's forbidden activity, the statement takes the force of an order: "Don't sit on the table, or else" (Sinclair and Coulthard, 1975).

In a similar manner, the meaning of instructional acts in this classroom was not conveyed by their grammatical form alone. The teacher received "answers" when she had not asked what would conventionally be called questions. For example, on many occasions the teacher began a sentence and paused, and the students completed her sentence, thereby producing an "answer."

Initiation	Reply	Evaluation
5:13 T: I called the tractor a "mmm . . ."	R: Machine.	
5:15 T: See the . . .	E: Slide.	

Other times the teacher's pause was accompanied by a gesture that produced an "answer."

Initiation	Reply	Evaluation
5:31 T: All right, and then . . . (pointing)	S: See the cafeteria.	
5:50 T: So this says . . . (holding up card)	Many: See.	

On other occasions the teacher received "answers" when she gave commands.

Initiation	Reply	Evaluation
5:16 T: It starts with that "ss" sound we were talking about yesterday.	A: Snake.	
5:49 T: Count them.	M: (counts numbers on board)	
5:97 T: Say it again, Miguel.	M: That's real when he was little.	

The implicit meaning of these utterances was not conveyed by their overt form because, as Hymes has put it, "one and the same sentence, the same set of words in the same syntactic relationship, may now be a request, now a command, now a complaint, now an insult, depending on tacit understanding within a community" (1972:xxviii). From the point of view of the functions of language in the classroom (Cazden, John, and Hymes, 1972), the teacher elicits information from students; she does not ask them questions. These observations reinforce the view that the study of language in naturally occurring situations requires the use of functional rather than grammatical concepts. For these reasons, terms like "initiations and replies," "elicitations and responses," are used here instead of grammatically based expressions like "questions and answers."

Furthermore, an elicitation does not seek just any information, it seeks particular information. In fact, four different kinds of elicitations were located in the instructional phase of these lessons: (1) choice elicitations, (2) product elicitations, (3) process elicitations, and (4) metaprocess elicitations.[3] Each of these initiation acts was followed by a specific kind of reply.

The choice elicitation calls upon the respondent to agree or disagree with a statement provided by the questioner. This type of elicitation contains the information that the respondent needs in order to form the reply. These elicitation acts are illustrated in the following segments of transcript. The first two examples are from a lesson in which the teacher was attempting to elicit the name of a story from the students.

Initiation	Reply	Evaluation
5:3 T: Is it about taking a bath?	Many: No.	
5:4 T: Is it about the sunshine?	Many: No.	

The next two examples are from a lesson in which the teacher asked the students to vote on options for one of many classroom procedures, which were written on the chalkboard.

Initiation	Reply	Evaluation
7:24 T: Now which one is that one?	Rafael: The middle one.	
7:25 T: The middle ones?	Rafael: (shakes head yes)	

These acts are called choice elicitations because the respondent need only agree or disagree with the teacher's statements, that is, choose a yes or no response (as in 5:3, 5:4, 7:25) or a response from a list provided by the teacher in the elicitation (as in 7:24).

The product elicitation asks respondents to provide a factual response such as a name, a place, a date, a color. The following example displays the teacher's search for correct factual information about sentences written about the schoolyard map.

Initiation	Reply	Evaluation
5:14 T: And then it says (points to fourth line) . . .	All: (no response)	
5:15 T: See the . . .	Edward: Slide.	
5:16 T: It starts with that "ss" sound we were talking about yesterday.	Audrey: Snake.	
5:17 T: See the . . .	__: Road. Edward: Road.	

The process elicitation asks for respondents' opinions or interpretations. This type is illustrated by two examples drawn from a lesson in which the teacher is asking the students to decide on a modification of classroom procedure.

Initiation	Reply	Evaluation
7:19 T: Jeannie, what do you think?	J: Uh, helping with the trays.	
7:25 T: Why do you like the middle one?	R: Cause they could take their own.	

Choice, product, and process elicitations ask for factual information, opinions, and interpretations. A fourth kind of elicitation asks students to be reflective about the process of making connections between elicitations and responses. These elicitations are called metaprocess elicitations because they ask students to formulate the grounds of their reasoning. They ask students to provide the rule or procedure by which they have arrived at or remembered answers. Metaprocess elicitations appear very infrequently in these materials (only 8 of 480, or 1 percent of all elicitations initiated by the teacher). Although students are not always successful in formulating the grounds of their reasoning, there may be pedagogical potential in having students become aware of the grounds of their reasoning, a prospect that Fisher (1976) considers.

The following example illustrates a successful attempt to have a student explain the basis upon which she arrived at an answer.

Initiation	Reply	Evaluation
8:15 T: And Carolyn, how did you remember where it was? It's kind of in the middle of the country and hard to find out.	C: Cuz, cuz, all three of the grandmothers (pause) cuz, cuz, Ms. Coles told us to find it and she said it started with an *a* and I said there (pointing) and it was right there.	

CLOSING THE LESSON   The completion of a lesson is a mirror image of its opening. While at the beginning of lessons, participants inform each other of what they are going to do, at their closing, they formulate what they have done.

As in the beginning of lessons, this formulation often takes the form of a soliloquy by the teacher. As an example, here is the teacher's final comment from the Namecards lesson:

Initiation	Reply	Evaluation
4:46		T: Well, I see we'll have to do a lot more work with those names so that you can learn to read them and can pass out books with people's names on them, and papers with people's names on them, and things like that.

The finale was often much shorter, with teacher and students jointly producing the closing verbally, as at the end of Whistle for Willy:

Initiation	Reply	Evaluation
4:141 Jerome: That's all.		T: That's all for this morning.

Directives preparing students for the next round of classroom activity are also found intertwined with these informatives:

Initiation	Reply	Evaluation
4:82 T: Um, ok, let's these four people take your chairs back to your seats.	Many: (return to seats)	T: No, not right now, Patricia.

Initiation	Reply	Evaluation
4:83 T: Oh, Mercedes, hold it, now put it down and pick it up and hold it the other way.		
4:84 Carolyn: From the back.		T: From the back, that's right, good.
4:85 T: Ok, take your chairs. Uh, ok, let's see, Edward, Rafael, Roberto and Everett.	Many: (return to seats)	
4:86 Carolyn: Edward, Rafael, Roberto, Everett.	Many: (return to seats)	
4:87 T: Ok, Alfredo, Martin, Jerome, Ernesto.	Many: (return to seats)	
4:88 Carolyn: Alfredo, Martin, Jerome, Ernesto.	Many: (return to seats)	
4:89 T: And now you.	Many: (return to seats)	
4:90 Sabrina: Teacher, you		

Initiation	Reply	Evaluation
forgot to put it back in my box.	T: Yes, I did.	
4:91. T: What's my name?	C: Um, Ms. Aycox, I mean Miss Cazden.	T: Ms. Cazden.
4:92 Sabrina: I already know your name.		T: Some of you do, some of you do.

SUMMARY   These classroom lessons are composed of three phases: an opening, an instructional, and a closing phase. Each phase serves a different function in lessons. Teachers and students inform each other that they are going to conduct a lesson and make procedural arrangements during the opening phase. Academic information is exchanged during the instructional phase. The closing phase is a mirror image of the opening phase. Here, teachers and students formulate what they have done, and prepare to move on to the next classroom activity.

Each phase is composed of distinctive interactional sequences. The opening phase is composed of directive and informative sequences. The directive calls for respondents to take procedural action, such as sharpening pencils, opening books, or moving to see the board in preparation for instruction. The informative passes on information, ideas, and opinions. It calls upon respondents to "pay attention." Elicitations exchange academic information. Hence, directives and informatives "frame" the elicitation of academic information that comprises the interior of lessons, thereby distinguishing lessons from other parts of the stream of ongoing behavior.

Interactional Sequences in Classroom Lessons

Each of the sequences discussed in the previous section was initiated by the teacher. Each initiation was followed by a reply from the students. More specifically, particular replies occurred with particular initiation acts. There were 480 exchanges initiated by the teacher in these lessons. The distribution of types of initiations and replies is shown in table 2.1. This distribution seems to indicate that specific reply acts occur in an obligatory relationship with specific initiation acts. Certain reply acts seem, in fact, to be *demanded* by certain initiation acts. A choice elicitation seems to demand a choice reply, a process elicitation compels the appearance of a process reply, and so on.

Co-occurrence relationships (Gumperz, 1964; Ervin-Tripp, 1972:324ff) are said to operate in everyday discourse such that the appearance of one form of informal speech (such as an informal address term) will be followed by the appearance of other informal ways of talking (for example, slang terms, elliptical constructions). The conversational forms that are related to each other by these co-occurrence rules often appear side by side. So, for example, a greeting offered by one person will be followed immediately by a greeting from another, a question will be followed immediately by an answer, an inquiry about states of health will be followed by "state of being" information. Hypothetical examples of these "adjacency pairs" (Sacks, Schegloff, and Jefferson, 1974) are easy to imagine. A conversation between speakers A and B, for example, might include a greeting pair (A: Hi. B: Hi.); a "state of health" pair (A: How are you? B: Fine, how are you?); and a question-answer pair (A: Do you have the time? B: Yes, it's two o'clock.).

These kinds of co-occurrence relationships seem to govern the interactional sequences in lessons as well, for particular kinds of replies follow particular kinds of initiation acts with great regularity. The symmetry established between initiation and reply acts by the co-occurrence rules operating in classroom lessons is as follows:

Initiation	Reply
choice elicitation	choice response
product elicitation	product response
process elicitation	process response

TABLE 2.1. THE DISTRIBUTION OF STUDENT REPLIES FOLLOWING TEACHER-INITIATED ACTS.

Teacher initiation	Student reply							
	Reaction	Acknowl-edgment	Choice response	Product response	Process response	Meta-process response	No reply	Other	Total
Directive	19	—	—	—	—	—	9	—	28
Informative	5	81	—	2	—	—	—	1	89
Choice elicitation	—	—	52	6	0	0	2	1	61
Product elicitation	1	—	0	232	0	0	32	14	279
Process elicitation	—	—	0	0	11	0	4	0	15
Metaprocess elicitation	—	—	1	0	0	4	2	1	8
Total	25	81	53	240	11	4	49	17	480

Initiation	Reply
metaprocess elicitation	metaprocess response
informative	acknowledgment
directive	reaction

Once an instructional sequence has been initiated, inter-action continues until the symmetry between initiation and reply acts is obtained. This symmetry is established in one of two ways. If the reply compelled by the initiation act appears in the next turn of talk, the result is a "three-part teacher-student sequence." The first part of the sequence is an initia-tion act, the second part is a reply act, and the third part is an evaluation act. If the reply called for by the initiation act does not appear in the next turn of talk, the initiator employs a number of strategies until the expected reply does appear. The result is an "extended sequence" of interaction.

THREE-PART INSTRUCTIONAL SEQUENCES Examples of the three-part teacher-student sequence are shown below. The first examples are from the Namecards lesson, in which the teacher asked students to identify the names of the students presented to them on cards.

Initiation	Reply	Evaluation
4:39 T: And whose is this?	Many: Veronica.	T: Oh, a lot of people knew that one.
4:45 T: Um, whose name is this?	L: Mercedes.	T: Mercedes, all right.

The second pair of examples is from the Map Words lesson, in which the teacher asked students to read the lines of a story displayed in front of them.

Initiation	Reply	Evaluation
5:77 T: Now who knows what this one says (holds up new card)? This is the long word. Who knows what it says?	A: Cafeteria.	T: Cafeteria, Audrey, good for you.
5:82 T: What does it say over there?	Many: Cafeteria.	T: That's right.

The third example is from the Cafeteria Trays lesson, in which the teacher asked the students to decide the best procedure for cleaning up after lunch.

Initiation	Reply	Evaluation
7:21 T: Um, why do you think that would be better than each child carrying his own?	J: Cause that's ah, that's a job for them.	T: Yes, it would be a job.

The fourth set of examples is from the Birthplaces lesson, in which the teacher posted students' families' birthplaces on a map on the bulletin board.

Initiation	Reply	Evaluation
8:5 T: Uh, Prenda, ah, let's see if we can		

Initiation	Reply	Evaluation
find, here's your name. Where were you born, Prenda?	P: San Diego.	T: You were born in San Diego, all right.
8:6 T: Um, can you come up and find San Diego on the map?	P: (goes to board and points)	T: Right there, okay.

As each elicitation act was completed by a reply from the students, the teacher positively evaluated the students' replies.

In effect, the three-part initiation-reply-evaluation sequence contains two coupled adjacency pairs. The initiation-reply is the first adjacency pair. When completed, this pair becomes the first part of a second adjacency pair. The second part of this pair is an act that positively evaluates the completion of the initiation-reply pair. These co-occurrence relationships can be visualized as follows:

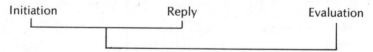

Initiation   Reply   Evaluation

The three-part sequential pattern predominates in teacher-initiated interaction in the nine lessons in this corpus. It characterizes the organization of directives and informatives as well as elicitations. Overall, 53 percent of all teacher-initiated sequences conform to this interactional pattern. The specific distribution of this pattern is summarized in table 2.2.

EXTENDED SEQUENCES OF INTERACTION   The reply called for does not always follow immediately after an initiation act. Sometimes students do not answer at all; sometimes they give partially complete answers; sometimes they answer incorrectly, or with an asymmetrical reply (that is, a "re-

TABLE 2.2. DISTRIBUTION OF THREE-PART
TEACHER-INITIATED SEQUENCES.

Type of initiation act	Total N	Number of three-part sequences	Percentage of three-part sequences
Elicitation	363	140	40
Informative	89	85	96
Directive	28	20	71
Total	480	245	53 (average)

sponse" when a "reaction" is in order). If the reply called for by the initiation act does not immediately appear in the next turn of talk, teacher-student interaction continues until symmetry between initiation and reply acts is established. The initiator employs a number of strategies, including (1) prompting incorrect or incomplete replies, (2) repeating, or (3) simplifying initiation acts until the reply called for by the original initiation act appears. The result is an extended sequence of interaction between teachers and students.

Prompting replies. The following instances illustrate the teacher's strategy of prompting after incorrect and partially correct replies. The first example is from the Map Words lesson. The teacher invited the students to read the lines of a story about the schoolyard map from a large poster. She pointed to the line of the story that said "See the machine."

Initiation	Reply	Evaluation
5:12 T: See the . . .	E: Tractors.	T: The, yes, tractors, it says mmm . . .
	E: Tractors.	T: It, it, but it is a tractor, but the word I wrote here, I didn't write tractor. But I wrote

Initiation	Reply	Evaluation
		a word that, another name for tractor that starts with "mm."
	P: Mmmmmm.	T: It starts with "mm," Patricia, yes.
5:13 T: I called the tractor a "mmm . . ."	R: Machine.	T: Machine, Rafael, good, I called it a machine.

The teacher, receiving incorrect replies ("tractors") and partially correct replies ("mmm"), continued questioning the students until she obtained a complete, correct reply.

Repeating elicitations. When students answered incorrectly, or did not answer at all, the teacher sometimes employed the strategy of not evaluating the reply while repeating the elicitation to the same or a different student, until she received a correct reply.

Many times in the Map Words lesson the students answered incorrectly when the teacher attempted to elicit recitations of the lines of the story. At such times, the teacher repeated her elicitation while indicating the line of the story they were to be reading.

Initiation	Reply	Evaluation
5:29 T: See (pause) the . . .	S: Tractor.	T: Yeah.
5:30 T: But what does it say instead of tractor?	__: Machine.	T: Machine.
5:31 T: Can you all say		

Initiation	Reply	Evaluation
that? Machine.	Many: Machine.	
5:32 T: See the machine. See the machine.	All: See the machine.	
5:33 T: But then it says, "see the . . ."	__: Cafeteria.	
5:34 T: But it starts with this now (points to 's') that we were talking about.	__: Street. P: Snake.	T: Street, good, like snake, Patricia, but it's street.

There are two topical concerns within this segment. The first involved reading the line of the story that said "See the machine" (5:29-5:32). The second involved reading the line of the story that said "See the street" (5:33-5:34). In both sequences, the teacher continued questioning the students without evaluation until a correct reply appeared.

Often when a student did not supply a correct reply, the teacher invited other students to help. One such instance of this practice appeared later in the Map Words lesson:

Initiation	Reply	Evaluation
5:71 T: Can somebody else find it again?	Many: (raise hands)	
5:72 T: Uh, Sabrina.	S: (points)	
5:73 T: Where else?		

Initiation	Reply	Evaluation
Edward, uh, Everett found this word that matches that, where else do you see that word?	S: (searches board)	
5:74 T: Who can help Sabrina?	Many: (raise hands)	
5:75 T: Uh, okay, Edward, come on.	E: (points)	T: Is that the same? Put it underneath.
5:76 T: Does it match?	Many: Yeah.	T: All right.

The teacher invited Edward (5:75) to help Sabrina match a word card to its equivalent on the storyboard. Note that the teacher did not evaluate Sabrina's incorrect reply; she neither prompted nor rejected this student's answer. Instead, she invited other students to provide the correct reply. A similar instance appears in the S and M Words lesson:

Initiation	Reply	Evaluation
3:41 T: What else, what else, Edward, what do you think we could put there that starts with an m?	C: (raises hand)	
3:42 T: Somebody in your family, Edward.	E: (shrugs shoulders no)	
3:43 T: All right, Jerome.	A: I know, I know.	

Initiation	Reply	Evaluation
	(raises hand)	
3:44 T: What?	A: Man.	T: Man, good for you, Audrey, that's a good one for here. Very good.

Edward declined answering the teacher's questions about a word that starts with *m* (3:42). The teacher did not evaluate that student's action; instead, she asked another student to supply the answer (3:43). When the correct answer appeared, the teacher positively evaluated it (3:44).

Simplifying elicitations. Besides prompting after incorrect and incomplete replies and repeating elicitations, the teacher also simplifies elicitations when she does not receive replies to her elicitation acts.

At the outset of the Map Words lesson, the teacher asked the students to name the story printed on the storyboard:

Initiation	Reply	Evaluation
5:1 T: Ok, what's the name of this story?	All: (no response)	
5:2 T: Who remembers, what's the name, what's the story about?	All: (no response)	
5:3 T: Is it about taking a bath?	Many: No.	
5:4 T: Is it about the sunshine?	Many: No.	

Initiation	Reply	Evaluation
5:5 T: Edward, what's it about?	E: The map.	T: The map. That's right, this says "the map."

Unable to obtain a reply (5:1 and 5:2), the teacher substituted a choice elicitation for a product elicitation (5:3, 5:4). Once the students responded to these simplified forms, she reverted to a product elicitation to obtain the information she wanted (5:5).

A similar sequence appeared in the Cafeteria Trays lesson. The teacher asked Victor to choose the procedure he preferred for cleaning up after lunch.

Initiation	Reply	Evaluation
7:13 T: What is, what is, uh, how would that work, Victor?	V: (no response)	
7:14 T: What would happen then? Which is the middle one?	V: (no response)	
7:15 T: Is that me taking all the trays?	M: (raises hand) V: (shakes head no)	
7:16 T: What, what is it?	V: _____	T: Each child you doing it, that's right. All right, wait a minute.

Unable to elicit process replies from Victor (7:13, 7:14), the teacher employed a choice elicitation (7:15). That is, the teacher reformulated the question so that the student could simply react to an option stated by the teacher rather than stating his own opinion directly. Once the teacher engaged the student in interaction, she employed a product elicitation (7:16). In this exchange, the student stated the name of the procedure he preferred. Thus, the teacher simplified a request for a stated opinion (process elicitation) to a request for agreement on a presented option (choice elicitation), and continued engaging the student until he named his option (product elicitation).

In a similar fashion, during the S and J Words lesson, the teacher asked Everett to indicate if the phrase "jumping jacks" began with the first letter of "Jerome" or "Sabrina."

Initiation	Reply	Evaluation
4:109 T: Everett, you remember, you suggested we do jumping jacks yesterday, remember?	E: Ah-ha.	
4:110 T: Does jumping jacks begin like Sabrina or like Jerome?	E: Sabrina	T: Say jumping jacks.
	E: Jump.	T: Jumping jacks.
4:111 T: Say J, J, say jumping jacks.	E: Jumping jacks.	T: All right, it's a, it's a beginning of the word jumping jacks.
4:112 T: Does that begin		

Initiation	Reply	Evaluation
like Sabrina or like Jerome?	E: (no response)	
4:113 T: Jumping . . .	E: Jerome.	T: Jerome, that's right.

When Everett answered incorrectly (4:110), the teacher broke the question down into simpler components (4:111), then prompted him until he replied to the original elicitation of information.

Each initiation act compels a certain type of reply. Once an initiation act has begun, interaction continues until symmetry between initiation and reply acts is established. If the reply called for by the initiation act appears in the very next turn of talk, the result is a three-part teacher-student sequence. If the reply called for by the initiation act does not immediately appear, the initiator "works" (prompts, repeats elicitations, simplifies initiations), until this symmetry is established. As soon as the students provide the reply that completes this symmetry, the teacher marks the completion of the extended sequence in the same way that she would mark the completion of a three-part sequence. She positively evaluates the content of these replies with such terms as "good for you" or "that's right," often while repeating the substance of students' replies. The result is an extended sequence of interaction.

The sequential organization of a typical extended sequence is displayed in the following diagram, in which braces indicate obligatory co-occurrence relationships:

Initiation	Reply	Evaluation
T: Elicits	Ss: Do not reply	
T: Repeats elicitation	Ss: Reply incorrectly	
T: Repeats elicitation	Ss: Reply incorrectly	T: Prompts
T: Repeats elicitation	Ss: Reply correctly	T: Accepts

In this hypothetical sequence, the teacher elicits information, but the students do not reply. The teacher repeats the initiation. This initiation is followed by an incorrect reply. A third initiation produces yet another incorrect reply. Then the teacher prompts and repeats the elicitation, which is followed by a correct reply. The teacher positively evaluates this reply, thereby ending the sequence.

In extended sequences, as in three-part sequences, co-occurence relationships bind initiation and reply acts and tie that completed exchange to the evaluation act. The co-occurrence relationships within these interactional sequences are "reflexively" established (Garfinkel, 1967; Garfinkel and Sacks, 1970). Given the first part of a sequence (an initiation act or an initiation-reply pair), the second part of the sequence (the reply act or the evaluation act) is "conditionally relevant" (Schegloff, 1968). That is, the appearance of the first part of a sequence makes the appearance of a second part prospectively possible. The actual appearance of the second part of the sequence gives meaning to the first part of the sequence.

The reflexive character of these sequences suggests that they have more in common with "social acts" (Mead, 1934) than with "speech acts" (Searle, 1969, 1976). Speech act theorists are critical of the formal semantics view of language (for example, Chomsky, 1965), which asserts that the function of language is the representation of thought, that the meaning of utterances is conveyed by grammatical distinctions and is determined by their truth value. However, certain speech act theorists (Searle, 1976; Sinclair and Coulthard, 1975) retain a version of the formal semantics notion of autonomous meaning. These speech act theorists say that the meaning of an utterance is determined by its illocutionary and perlocutionary force, not its grammatical features. And they maintain that this information is to be found within the internal structure of a given speech act. The autonomous view of meaning implies that speech acts are complete in themselves; that one need not look beyond the boundaries of the speech act to determine its meaning.

A social act, by contrast, requires the cooperative completion of an activity by the participants involved. Mead's description (1934) of a prototypical "conversation of gestures" exemplifies this point of view. The social act begins when one person gestures (for example, points) and ends when another person responds (looks in the direction of the point). The response (looking) completes the social act that was begun by the pointing gesture. The completion of the social act provides the meaning of the gesture that started the act.

The initiation-reply-evaluation acts of teacher-student interaction in these lessons seem to share these "prospective" and "retrospective" features (Schutz, 1962; Garfinkel, 1967; Cicourel, 1973). Any given act has a range of potential meanings. Its actual meaning is not known until the entire sequence is completed. The meaning of an act initiated by the teacher, for example, is prospective. Its actual meaning is realized retrospectively, when the act performed by the student is evaluated by the teacher. Likewise, the status of a student's reply as answer or nonanswer is not determined until the teacher contributes an evaluation.

Thus, individual acts of speech are not autonomous. The meaning of a given speech act is not contained within its internal structure. Instead, meaning resides in the reflexive assembly of initiation, reply, and evaluation acts into interactional sequences.

This finding suggests that a third act, evaluation, plays a significant role in instructional discourse. While evaluation seldom occurs in everyday discourse, it is an essential component of an instructional sequence. It contributes information about the initiator's intended meaning to the negotiation of a mutually acceptable reply. This finding also suggests that positive evaluation and negative evaluation of students do not fulfill equivalent functions. When students answer correctly, they receive positive evaluation. The positive evaluation is a terminal act; it marks the final boundary of a sequence, ending one and signaling that another is to begin. When students answer incorrectly, or incompletely, or not at all, they may or may not receive prompting or negative evaluation. Thus, negative evaluation, prompting, and nonevaluation are continuation acts; they do not appear at the end of teacher-student sequences, only in their interior.

Their function is to keep the interaction moving until symmetry between initiation and reply acts is established.

TOPICALLY RELATED SETS   Describing the sequential progression of directives, informatives, and elicitations from the beginning to the end of lessons is not enough. If stopped at this point, the analysis would not capture the overall organization of lessons.

This project benefited from an insightful teacher-as-researcher. As Cazden reminded us at a research meeting, the teacher does not elicit information from students randomly. Indeed, as it turns out, elicitation sequences are organized into larger units. And these units seem to be organized around topics. These larger organizational units are called topically related sets.

A topically related set is composed of a basic sequence, which establishes the topic for discussion. Basic sequences are often followed by one or more "conditional sequences," which build on the topic introduced in the basic sequence.

Since conditional sequences do not always appear after basic sequences, they are optional. They never appear alone. When they do appear, they appear only after a basic sequence has been completed. It is in this way that they are conditional: their appearance is dependent upon the prior appearance of a basic sequence.

The beginning of topically related sets.   The appearance of a topically related set is signaled by a unique combination of verbal, paralinguistic, and kinesic behavior. The beginnings of topically related sets were most notably marked by the teacher's orientation toward the instructional materials to be used. If the teacher was working with materials at the chalkboard, map, or storyboard, she shifted position toward that material and pointed to the topic of discussion. She established that orientational position vis à vis the students and instructional materials at the beginning of an elicitation sequence and maintained it throughout the duration of a topically related set. If she was working with hand-held materials, she either held up those materials or laid them on the floor in front of the students for the duration of a topically related set.

This postural shift was accompanied by verbal and paralinguistic behavior that further served to mark these distinctive units. The beginnings of topically related sets were marked by the appearance of a closed set of verbal forms that appear at no other places in lessons. This set includes "uh," "now," "okay," "um, now, um," "but," "uh now," "uh, let's see," and "and last of all." These verbal markers were often produced in a sharp staccato tone. The cadence of the teacher's voice quickened as she initiated a new topical set.

Basic sequences. Each topically related set contains a basic sequence in which the instructional topic of the lesson is introduced. The topic of basic sequences in each of the lessons is as follows:

S & M Words; S & J Words: Identification of words that start with letter designated by teacher on chalkboard.

Namecards: Identification of names of children held up on cards in front of children at the circle.

The Map: Location of objects that children had observed during a walk around the schoolyard on a map hung on the classroom wall at the circle.

Whistle for Willy: Identification of the number of students who could listen to a story on headphones.

Map Words: In the first part of this lesson, the recitation of lines of a story about the schoolyard map posted on a storyboard at the rug. In the second part, the location of a word from a pile on the floor, and matching it to its equivalent on the storyboard.

Cafeteria Trays: Elicitation of students' choices of procedure to solve a classroom problem; conducted at the chalkboard.

Birthplaces: Locating each student's and each student's family members' places of birth on a map hung on the classroom wall at the circle.

Martin Luther King Story: Eliciting information from students after reading lines of the story; conducted at the circle.

In some lessons (S and J Words, S and M Words, Whistle for Willy, and Martin Luther King Story), discussion of the basic topic ceased at the end of one structural sequence with one student, and a new round of discussion about that same topic was taken up with another student. In the other lessons, the participants expanded upon the topic introduced in the basic sequence, thereby creating a conditional sequence.

Conditional sequences. Expansions of basic topics via conditional sequences appear in five of the nine lessons in the corpus: Namecards, Map, Map Words, Cafeteria Trays, and Birthplaces lessons.

In the Map lesson, after the teacher asked the students to identify on the map the objects they had observed during their walk (4:52-54; 4:56-59; 4:67-69; 4:79), the teacher sometimes followed up this basic topic with requests to locate objects on the map (4:55; 4:60-64; 4:70-75; 4:80), and with discussions about the objects (4:65-66; 4:77-78).

On every occasion of questioning in the Namecards lesson, the teacher had a student identify the name on the flashcard she held in front of the class (4:4-6; 4:9-11; 4:14-18; 4:22-23; 4:25-27; 4:30-34; 4:36-37; 4:39; 4:42-43; 4:45-46). On some occasions, that terminated the topically related set (4:30-34; 4:36-37; 4:39; 4:45-46). On other occasions, especially at the beginning of the lesson, she had the student who identified the namecard link the name with the student in the class (4:12) or explain how he or she knew the answer to the original question (4:7). If either of those two options had been exercised, the teacher then confirmed the identification of the card with its owner.

In the second part of the Map Words lesson, the teacher employed a recurrent pattern of elicitation acts to match word cards to the storyboard. In each case, the teacher invited the student to (a) locate a card (5:37-39; 5:57; 5:66-68; 5:69-77; 5:84-89; 5:90); (b) place the card on the storyboard (5:41; 5:63-65; 5:78-82; 5:88), and (c) identify the word (5:54; 5:62; 5:77 and 83; 5:89). On some but not all occasions, the teacher also sought confirmation from the class (5:42), asked other students to repeat the same operation (5:69-76), or counted the number of similar words (5:43-46; 5:47-48; 5:51).

On each occasion of interaction with a student on the topic of choosing a solution to the cafeteria trays problem, the teacher asked a student to identify an alternative (7:6-10; 7:19-21; 7:23-25). On some, but not all occasions, the teacher then also asked that student to describe the operation of that procedure (7:13-16) and to explain why it was the preferred alternative (7:17; 7:22; 7:26-27).

In the Birthplaces lesson, the teacher's pattern of elicitations included determining each student's (or family member's) birthplace, locating that place on the map, and placing that information on the map. In addition to these basic sequences, the teacher and students sometimes engaged in discussions about the relative distances between cities (8:30-33; 8:34; 8:71-76; 8:127), and the bases of students' knowledge (8:12-14; 8:15-16; 8:126; 8:133).

The kinesic and paralinguistic markers, established at the outset of basic sequences, are continued throughout these conditional sequences. The teacher continued her orientation toward the students and materials throughout. The cadence of her voice, which had quickened at the opening of the basic sequence, continued at an even pace throughout the series of conditional sequences. In fact, the seams between basic and conditional sequences are virtually indistinguishable. There is no significant time gap between the two. The tempo of talk does not alter. There is no change in the way educational material is displayed. For all intents and purposes, the basic and conditional sequences blend into one interactional unit.

The ending of topically related sets. The closings of topically related sets are marked in ways that are similar to their openings. A finite set of verbal markers, which includes "all right" and "that's right," often with the correct reply repeated, appears only at the final juncture of topically related sets. The cadence of the teacher's presentation slows as she pronounces these words. Certain postural shifts occur simultaneously with verbal and paralinguistic boundary markers. She lowers presented materials, removes her hand from indicated material.

A REPRESENTATIVE EXAMPLE   The organization of elicitation sequences into basic and dependent sequences, and the
organization of these sequences into topically related sets is
a characteristic of all the lessons in this corpus. This hierarchical arrangement is particularly well displayed in the
Namecards lesson:

Initiation	Reply	Evaluation
4:9 T: Who knows whose namecard this is? (holds up namecard)	P: Mine. C: (raises hand)	T: Ah, if you see, if it's your namecard don't give the secret away if you, if . . .
4:10 T: Let's see, I'll just take some of the people who are here. Um, if it's your namecard, don't give away the secret. Whose namecard, who could tell us whose namecard this is? (holds card up)	C: (raises hand)	
4:11 T: Carolyn.	C: Patricia.	
4:12 T: Can you point to Patricia?	C: (points to Patricia)	T: That's right.
4:13 T: Is this your namecard?	P: (nods yes)	

Initiation	Reply	Evaluation
4:14 T: Whose namecard is this? Now, don't give away the secret if it's yours, don't give away the secret if it's yours, give other children a chance to look. (holds up name-card)		

The teacher held up a namecard for identification (4:9). When Patricia identified her own card, the teacher gave further instructions and held up the card again (4:10). When Carolyn identified the namecard correctly (4:11), the teacher asked her to locate that student (4:12) in the room, and then asked Patricia to confirm the identification. The identification of the namecard (4:9-11) is a basic sequence, which establishes the topic. The linking of the card to the person (4:12) and the confirmation of that identification (4:13) are conditional sequences, that is, their appearance is dependent upon the prior appearance of the basic identification of the namecard.

As soon as that information was provided, the teacher lowered the namecard while saying "that's right." The cadence of the teacher's voice changed from an even to a slowed presentation as she pronounced these words. The lowered namecard, the slowed cadence, and the "that's right" all mark the end of this topically related set of sequences.

At the completion of this topical set, another is begun (4:14). The teacher raised another card and quickened the pace of her voice as she asked students to identify the name on the card. That topical set contained a number of extended sequences, as students provided partially correct replies (4:15-16; 4:17) and had trouble locating the name on the card on a list posted on the board (4:19-21). One topical set follows another throughout the rest of the lesson.

The teacher often takes time to rearrange student seating (4:41), to greet tardy students (5:27-32; 4:115; 5:59), and to make other procedural readjustments (5:59-61; 5:86; 7:37) during lessons. She also provides further information about the course of the lesson while it is in progress. For example, she directed the attention of students from S to M words (3:38), drew new objects on the map of the schoolyard (4:60; 4:62; 4:67; 4:78), wrote new instructions on the board (4:100), changed the focus of the lesson from lines about the map story to individual words (5:37), reminded students of that task (5:84), and informed students of the different voting procedures (7:5; 7:30; 7:41).

It is important to note that these redirections of students' attention, procedural readjustments, and information about changes in instructional materials or focus appear in the break or juncture between the end of one topically related set and the beginning of another, and not within topically related sets. The presence of these directive and informative sequences at the boundaries and not in the interior of topically related sets produces further evidence of the integrity of these units as meaningful components of lessons.

The instructional phase of this and other lessons, then, is a progression of topically related sets. Teacher and students assemble one set after another from the opening of the instructional phase to its closing. Topically related sets, in turn, are composed of a sequence of basic (and sometimes conditional) sequences. Participants in these lessons mark the integrity of this hierarchical organization, verbally, paralinguistically, and kinesically.

Conclusions

The methodological goal of this book is to describe the social organization of classroom lessons, and to do so in such a way that the analysis is comprehensive and can be retrieved from the materials, so that the analysis is exhaustive. The nine lessons from this classroom are organized sequentially and hierarchically.

The sequential and hierarchical organization of those classroom events formulated by participants and researchers alike as "lessons" is displayed in figure 2.1. Included in this figure are the major lesson components. They are displayed vertically, with the smallest unit at the bottom and the largest at the top. Sequential arrangements are displayed horizontally, with the first in the sequence on the left and the last in the sequence on the right.

In contrast to correlational studies of the classroom, which only tabulate the frequency of occurrence of teacher and student behavior, thereby treating behavior in isolation, the analysis here is holistic. Teacher and student behavior, verbal and nonverbal behavior, have been treated as parts of an integrated interactional system.

In contrast to participant observation studies of classrooms, which provide anecdotal, albeit compelling evidence, this is a comprehensive analysis with retrievable data. The schema presented (figure 2.1) is descriptive of the structure of each and every lesson in this corpus. The grounds of the interpretation are presented along with instructions for locating materials in the transcribed corpus.

The sequential organization of lessons. Looked at from beginning to end, classroom lessons are alternations of verbal and nonverbal behavior between teachers and students. The most recurrent pattern is for the teacher to act, and then the students to act, and then the teacher, and so on. These alternations of behavior are assembled into interactional sequences jointly produced by teachers and students. Each sequence has three parts: an initiation act, a reply act, and an evaluation act. An act initiated by one classroom participant, most frequently the teacher, is followed by a reply, most often by the students, which in turn is followed by an evaluation act. These pieces of interaction are sequences in the sense that one action follows another with great regularity. These sequences are distinctively interactional in that they involve the cooperative completion of activity by the participants involved. That is, teacher and students work in concert to assemble interactional sequences.

These interactional sequences occur in specific places in lessons. Directives and informatives occur at the beginning

FIGURE 2.1. THE STRUCTURE OF CLASSROOM LESSONS.

Event	Lesson							
Phase	Opening		Instructional				Closing	
Type of sequence	Directive	Informative	Topical sets		Topical sets		Informative	Directive
			Elicit	Elicit	Elicit	Elicit		
Organization of sequences	I-R-E	$I\text{-}R(^{E}_{\emptyset})$	I-R-E	I-R-E	I-R-E	I-R-E	$I\text{-}R(^{E}_{\emptyset})$	I-R-E
Participants	T-S-T	T-S-T	T-S-T	T-S-T	T-S-T	T-S-T	T-S-T	T-S-T

⟶ Sequential organization ⟶

⟵ Hierarchical organization

Key: T = teacher; S = student; I-R-E = initiation-reply-evaluation sequence; $(^{E}_{\emptyset})$ = Evaluation optional in informative sequence.

and ending of lessons, while elicitations occur in the middle. It is on this basis that phases in lessons can be distinguished. Directives and informatives make up the opening and closing phases, while elicitations make up the instructional phase of lessons.

Interactional sequences serve different functions in classroom interaction. Directives engage participants in the giving and receiving of procedural and preparatory instructions. Elicitations engage participants in the exchange of academic information about factual matters, opinions, interpretations, or the grounds of their reasoning. Informatives present information to participants, most notably formulating what is to happen and what has happened in lessons.

Hierarchical organization. Looked at from bottom to top, lessons are organized into interactional units of increasing size. Initiation, reply, and evaluation acts are assembled into elicitation, informative, or directive interactional sequences. Interactional sequences are arranged into topical sets. Topical sets, in turn, make up the instructional phase of lessons, and a sequence of phases composes the classroom event called a lesson.

The hierarchical arrangement of the components of lessons is displayed in figure 2.2. This figure is meant to be read from the bottom line, representing the smallest unit of analysis, to the top line, representing the largest unit of analysis.

These relationships can also be displayed as recursive "rewrite rules," from the most general component to the most specific, as in figure 2.3.

FIGURE 2.2. THE HIERARCHICAL ARRANGEMENTS OF LESSONS.

Phase + Phase + Phase ⟶	Lesson
TRS + TRS + TRS ⟶	Phase
BX + CS ⟶	Topically Related Set (TRS)
IS + IS ⟶	Basic or Conditional Sequence (BS, CS)
Initiation + Reply + Evaluation ⟶	Instructional Sequence (IS)

FIGURE 2.3. LESSON COMPONENTS DISPLAYED AS
REWRITE RULES.

Lesson ⟶ Opening Phase + Instructional Phase + Closing Phase
Opening, Closing Phase ⟶ Directive + Informative
Instructional Phase ⟶ TRS + TRS
TRS ⟶ Basic + Conditional Sequence (or Interactional Sequence)
Instructional Sequence ⟶ Initiation + Reply + Evaluation

These recursive rules are analogous to a grammar, although the use of that term here should not be confused with its use in linguistic analysis. For example, the goal of generative-transformational linguistics (Chomsky, 1965) has been to produce a grammar that would account for all syntactically, semantically, and phonologically correct sentences while excluding all ungrammatical ones. The goal of constitutive analysis, on the other hand, is to produce a grammar that accounts for the structure of social events.

The unit of analysis in generative-transformational theory is the sentence, while the unit of analysis for constitutive studies is the event. While considering the sentence as the unit of analysis makes an investigation psychological or individualistic in nature, a focus on events moves the investigation to a social or interactional plane. Sentences are produced by a person, while people participate in social events. Sentences are primarily linguistic phenomena, while events are constellations of verbal and nonverbal behavior made manifest in practical circumstances. So, despite a common concern with producing systematic, even formal descriptions, these two approaches are significantly different in their phenomena of interest and units of analysis.

Reflexive tying structures. While all interactional sequences in these lessons are reflexively tied together, these co-occurrence relationships take different forms in three-part and extended sequences. They link adjacent initiation and reply acts in three-part sequences. They range across a considerable stretch of discourse in extended sequences. Because the reply that completes an initiation act may not appear until many turns later, not all teacher-student sequences are composed of two adjacently related pairs. The existence of extended sequences demonstrates that co-occurrence operates across considerable stretches of interaction. This suggests that the reflexive structures that tie interactional sequences together are wide-ranging and not limited to adjacently occurring utterances. Instead, adjacent sequences are a variety of reflexively tied sequences, a category that also includes delayed, nonadjacent (compare Goffman, 1975:36; Philips, 1976:93), elliptically coupled (Merritt, 1977), and extended sequences.

Furthermore, the principles of reflexive tying, first located as alternations of behavior united into interactional sequences, are recapitulated at increasing levels of lesson organization. Just as a series of initiation-reply-evaluation acts reflexively makes up an elicitation, directive, or informative interactional sequence, and a series of sequences makes up a topically related set, so too a series of topical sets reflexively makes up the instructional phase of lessons, and a sequence of phases composes the classroom event called the lesson.

The overwhelming pervasiveness of reflexive tying leads me to believe that this structure, which establishes symmetry within three-part and extended interactional sequences, is a basic organizational structure of classroom lessons. Reflexive tying not only contributes to the social organization of interactional sequences, it seems to be the glue that binds entire interactional events together.

Because reflexive tying operates across extended sequences of interaction, teacher-student interaction does not appear to be under immediate stimulus control. Instead, the machinery governing teacher-student interaction in classroom lessons seems to be more akin to an interactional model than to a stochastic model (see, for example, Mishler, 1975a, 1975b).

A stochastic model of behavior is Markovian in nature. It assumes that the next event is affected most by the immediately prior event. An interactional model recognizes, first of all, that behavior can be influenced by immediately prior events, those in the distant past, and those that have yet to occur. Each observed behavior between teacher and student is a function of the interconnected behaviors that retrospectively precede it in time and those that are prospectively possible. An interactional model recognizes, secondly, that behavior between participants is not unidirectional, it is reciprocal. Students not only are influenced by the teacher, they influence the teacher in turn.

Participants' orientation to the structure of lessons. The sequential and hierarchical organization of lessons described in this chapter was derived from an extensive analysis of videotapes and transcripts from the nine lessons in the corpus of materials. It is a contention of this analysis that this machinery is not just a researcher's analytic apparatus, but that it guides the participants in the course of their interactions together.

Participants demonstrated their orientation toward each sequential and hierarchical component of lessons. The lesson as a classroom event was set apart from other classroom events by large-scale shifts in position and physical rearrangements. At the beginning and ending of lessons, the participants moved in and out of the two instructional centers. Either the students sat at their desks facing the teacher who was standing at the chalkboard, or the teacher and students sat in a circle facing each other. If the lesson took place at the chalkboard, the teacher shifted to a stationary standing position. If the lesson took place at the rug, the teacher shifted from a standing to a sitting position. Students assumed quiet, attentive poses facing the teacher. Lessons took place only when all other instructional material was put away; for example, students cleared their desks of all books, pencils, paper. At the close of lessons, these shifts were reversed. The group moved to another part of the room, thereby shifting from sitting to standing positions.

The boundaries between the phases in lessons were likewise marked in significant ways. The physical arrangements and positioning of the participants remained constant throughout all phases of the lesson, with momentary exceptions while students went to the board, map, or chart. Teacher directions and informatives, spoken in natural conversational rhythm, made their unique appearance in the opening and closing phases, while the materials to be used in the lesson were introduced in the transition from the opening to the instructional phase.

The boundary between the instructional phase and the closing phase was a mirror image of that between the opening phase and the instructional phase. Materials were removed, and informatives formulating what had taken place and teacher directives transporting the group to the next event occurred here.

Participants demonstrated their orientation to the topical coherence of lessons verbally, paralinguistically, and kinesically. The beginnings of topically oriented sets were marked by the appearance of verbal forms that appeared at no other places in lessons. These verbal markers were often produced in a sharp, staccato tone. The cadence of the initiator's voice quickened as a new topical set was initiated. It slowed to normal conversational rhythm in the interior of basic sequences. This normal rhythm was maintained throughout the conditional sequences that composed a given set. These verbal and paralinguistic markers were accompanied by postural shifts. The teacher oriented her body toward the educational materials used within a given topically related set.

The closings of topically related sets were marked in equivalent ways. A finite set of verbal markers that often accompanied the repetition of the correct reply appeared only at the final juncture of topically related sets. The cadence of the teacher's presentation slowed as she pronounced these words. Her body shifted as well. She lowered presented material or removed her hands from it. These postural shifts occurred simultaneously with paralinguistic and verbal boundary markers.

The completion of an instructional sequence begun by an initiation act was most noticeably marked by an evaluation act. The teacher began the sequence with an initiation act. If the reply demanded appeared in the next immediate turn of talk, the result was a three-part sequence. The first part of the sequence was an initiation, the second part was a reply. These acts formed an adjacency pair. This pair then became the first part of a second adjacency pair, the second part of which was an evaluation act that commented on the completion of the initiation-reply pair. If the reply demanded by the initiation did not immediately appear, teacher-student interaction continued across a number of turns. The participants engaged in interactional work until the reply was obtained. The result was an extended sequence of interaction, the completion of which is marked in the same way as the completion of a three-part sequence: by a positive evaluation.

This boundary-marking work makes these sequential and hierarchical units organizational features of classroom lessons for both participants and researchers. The presence of these markers demonstrates that classroom interaction (compare McDermott, 1976; Erickson and Shultz, 1977), like counseling sessions (Erickson and Shultz, 1978) and psychiatric sessions (Kendon, 1970; Scheflen, 1972), is a rhythmic, cooperative activity involving the timing of gesture and speech. Interaction is segmented, and to some extent controlled, by participants' systematically changing arrays of postural configurations. Proxemic shifts, tempo changes, and unique lexical entries are all structurally important. They function to demarcate the continuous flow of interaction into more discrete segments. These configurations have implications for what is communicated. They indicate that something new is happening. Students, especially, must be aware of the signaling value that postural shifts, conversational rhythm, and prosody have on lesson content. As I will show in chapter 4 (and has been demonstrated elsewhere; see, for example, Byers and Byers, 1972; Erickson and Shultz, 1978; McDermott, 1976), successful interaction occurs when teachers and students synchronize the rhythm of gesture and speech with each other, while breakdowns in communication occur in the absence of this synchrony.

Students' contributions to lessons. Interaction in these lessons is not initiated exclusively by the teacher. Students as well as the teacher elicit information, give directives, and provide information during lessons. Table 2.3 summarizes the frequency of teacher- and student-initiated acts in the nine lessons. As the table shows, both teachers and students initiate action, although the teacher does so much more frequently than the students do.

TABLE 2.3. FREQUENCY OF TEACHER- AND STUDENT-INITIATED SEQUENCES (TOTAL NUMBER OF SEQUENCES = 590).

Teacher-initiated sequences	Number	%	Student-initiated sequences	Number	%
Elicitation	361	61.2	Elicitation	26	4.0
Informative	89	15.2	Informative	72	12.0
Directive	28	4.5	Directive	10	1.6
Other	2	0.3	Other	2	0.3
Total	480	81.1	Total	110	17.9

In addition to a simple numerical difference, there are important interactional differences between teacher- and student-initiated sequences. First of all, the sequential organization of many student-initiated actions is different from that of teacher-initiated actions. Furthermore, student-initiated sequences are not evenly distributed across the corpus of materials. They occurred more often at the end of the year than at the beginning, indicating a change in the social organization of the lessons through time. Finally, they are not randomly distributed within a given lesson. Significantly, those that disrupt the course of the lesson occur within the boundaries of a topically related set, while those that influence the course of the lesson occur at the junctures between topical sets.

These quantitative differences and interactional features suggest that student-initiated action be discussed as a topic in its own right. An extended discussion of this topic is, therefore, reserved for chapter 4.

3 THE STRUCTURING OF CLASSROOM LESSONS

The Problem of Order
in the Classroom

FOR SOCIOLOGISTS, the problem of social order is a paramount theoretical concern. Teachers, especially beginning teachers, often report a similar, though more practical, concern for social order (Dunkin and Biddle, 1974: 134). This practical concern is often expressed in terms of student discipline and classroom management.

This concern for order is not necessarily an end in itself: it is more of a means to an end. It is a utilitarian stance adopted for the practical purposes of achieving educational objectives, which include academic and interpersonal issues, intertwined with matters of social control. These objectives may be talked about as being on a teacher's agenda.

Observation in classrooms and discussions with teachers show that some items on the teacher's agenda are global and encompass the whole year, while others may be so specific that they focus on only a single lesson. Some of the more global objectives concern students' academic development. Here the goal is improvement in students' ability to read, write, compute, and so on during the course of the year. Other items on the teacher's agenda concern social adjustment. Here the goal is growth in students' respect for each other and in their understanding of the world around them during the course of the year.

Classroom activities are also organized to deal with more specific goals on the teacher's agenda. Teachers often plan "academic units," integrated sets of lessons organized around certain topics, to achieve more specific ends. For example, a set of lessons in a social studies unit might be arranged in conjunction with Black History Week. At such times, the teacher's objective is that the students gather some general impressions and ideas by the end of the unit, for example, that they acquire more sensitivity to people of different cultural backgrounds.

The teacher's agenda also includes a number of short-term objectives that are specific to any one school day or one lesson. In a lesson, the teacher wants to teach some specific material in a limited time frame. At such times, the teacher is concerned that students have equivalent opportunities for expression and development. The global and intermediate-range agenda items form a background for the immediate concerns of any lesson.

The teacher's project, then, is to complete the objectives on her agenda and to do so in an orderly way. This project is entangled in a web of practical circumstances. The most overwhelming circumstance is the raw number of students who often make simultaneous and competing demands for the teacher's attention.

Other practicalities often interfere with the accomplishment of immediate agenda objectives. Classroom lessons and other activities are constantly interrupted. Some of these interruptions originate within the classroom. Students are ill or tardy. Equipment fails to work. Aides are reassigned. Others originate outside the classroom. Unexpected visitors, loudspeaker announcements, fire drills interrupt the flow of classroom activity. Educational specialists often enter classrooms to present special events, to test students, or to remove them from the class for enrichment programs. These interruptions disrupt the continuity of instruction, which is organized hour by hour, day by day.

When disruption occurs, considerations associated with social control often take precedence over more academic concerns. Teachers talk about these times with expressions like "keeping the lid on," "just maintaining," and the like. The influence of practical circumstances on educational objectives suggests that often a basic item on a teacher's agenda is "getting through the day."

In chapter 2 I described the structure of lessons in terms of their hierarchical and sequential arrangements. That analysis describes what the organization of classroom lessons is, but it does not reveal how that organization comes about. In this chapter I pursue that issue by examining what teachers and students do that produces the organized character of classroom lessons.

Social organization has been described as an interactional accomplishment (Garfinkel, 1967; Cicourel, 1968; Scheflen, 1972); that is, people act together to assemble the organized character of social events.

This conception of action suggests that classroom participants engage in interactional work to assemble the organized character of classroom events such as lessons. Applying this conception to the organization of classroom lessons, the *structuring* of classroom lessons becomes the topic of inquiry. This inquiry shows that the teacher and students engage in a "turn-allocation machinery" that achieves the orderly progression of interaction in lessons. This turn-allocation machinery consists of two sets of procedures: the basic turn-allocation procedures, and improvisational strategies. The former set operates under normal classroom conditions. However, the practical circumstances of the classroom dictate that the teacher, in her role as organizer of classroom lessons, also have access to methods for organizing interaction that are responsive to spontaneous, unexpected, emergent occurrences. Methods that operate when practical circumstances intervene are referred to as improvisational strategies.

The primary focus of this chapter is on the procedures used to achieve the teacher's agenda during lessons. As a result, this description may seem to relegate the students' role to fitting into the teacher's agenda. But we cannot forget that students have objectives they wish to reach during the course of a classroom event, a school day, or a school year. An adequate description of students' competence in the classroom captures the students' skills in accomplishing their own agendas. Some of the procedures that students employ to achieve their objectives will be explored in chapter 4.

Achieving Order under Normal Classroom Circumstances

The organization of classroom lessons is achieved through the operation of a turn-allocation machinery. This turn-allocation machinery is a part of each initiation act. As described in chapter 2, each interactional sequence exchanges information (elicitations), gives information (informatives), or gives procedural instructions (directives). The analysis in this chapter shows that an interactional sequence not only specifies the action to be taken but also does the work of identifying the population of people who are to reply to the initiation.

BASIC TURN-ALLOCATION PROCEDURES Under normal classroom conditions, respondents are selected in one of three ways: by individual nominations, by invitations to bid, or by invitations to reply. The person or group of persons who is to respond to each initiation is identified by these procedures. This collection of procedures contributes to the structuring of classroom lessons.

Individual nomination. One turn-allocation procedure involves the teacher nominating a particular next speaker by name:

Initiation	Reply	Evaluation
8:5 T: Where were you born, Prenda?	P: San Diego.	T: You were born in San Diego, all right.

In this example, the teacher called upon Prenda by name as part of the initiation act. This act serves to allocate the floor to Prenda, to indicate that it is her turn to reply.

Individual students were not always nominated verbally. Sometimes a particular next speaker was nominated by nonverbal means. The teacher pointed to students she wanted to reply, nodded her head at them, or maintained eye contact with them. Often the nonverbal means of speaker selection occurred after she had named a particular student. She then held the floor for that student while engaging in a series of follow-up exchanges:

Initiation	Reply	Evaluation
7:20 T: Jeannie, what do you think?	J: Uh, helping with the trays. R: (lowers hand)	
7:21 T: You'd, you'd like to have some children, say two children, carry all the trays on Monday and another two carry them all on Wednesday?	J: (shakes her head yes) R: (raises hand)	
7:22 T: Um, why do you think that would be better than each child carrying his own?	J: Cause that's a, that's a job for them.	T: Yes, it would be a job.
7:23 T: Roberto, what do you think?	R: (lowers hand, points) That one.	
7:24 T: Now which, which one is that one?	R: The middle one.	
7:25 T: The middle ones?	R: (shakes head yes)	
7:26 T: Why do you like		

Initiation	Reply	Evaluation
the middle one?	R: Cause they could take their own.	T: Because what?
	R: They could take their own.	
7:27 T: You like to be able to take your own?	R: (shakes head yes)	T: All right.

This example shows that the teacher held the floor for Jeannie (7:21-22) and Roberto (7:24-27) by orienting her body toward the students and maintaining eye contact with each of them.

Another example of the nonverbal form of the individual nomination turn-allocation procedure appeared in the *S* and *J* Words lesson:

Initiation	Reply	Evaluation
4:109 T: Everett, you remember you suggested we do jumping jacks yesterday, remember?	E: Ah-ha.	
4:110 T: Does jumping jacks begin like Sabrina or like Jerome? (touches board)	E: Sabrina.	T: Say jumping jacks.
	E: Jump . . .	T: Jumping jacks.
4:111 T: Say J, J, say jumping jacks.	E: Jumping jacks.	T: All right.

Initiation	Reply	Evaluation
		It's a, it's a beginning of the word jumping jacks.
4:112 T: Does that begin like Sabrina or like Jerome?	E: (no response)	
4:113 T: Jumping . . .	E: Jerome.	T: Jerome, that's right.

In this exchange, the teacher left her place at the front of the entire class and moved closer to Everett. She maintained eye contact and faced him to the exclusion of the rest of the class throughout the exchange.

These ways of allocating the floor to the next speaker represent the individual nomination turn-allocation procedure. This procedure is shown in figure 3.1, using the teacher elicitation as a typical initiation act. The individual nomination procedure operates in the following way: the teacher elicits information; provides a directive or offers information; and

FIGURE 3.1. THE INDIVIDUAL NOMINATION
TURN-ALLOCATION PROCEDURE.

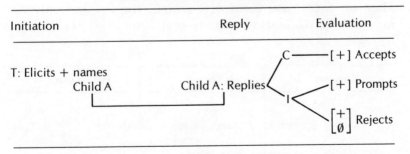

Key: C = correct reply; I = incorrect reply; Ø = no evaluation.

simultaneously names the student who is to respond. The speaker nominated in the initiation now has the floor. It is that person's turn to reply. After the student replies, the teacher evaluates content of the reply. If the reply is correct, the teacher positively evaluates it; if the reply is incorrect, the teacher employs various continuation strategies. She either prompts, rejects, or repeats the elicitation until a correct reply is obtained (see chapter 2).

The individual nomination procedure is a constituent feature of what Griffin and Humphrey (1978) have called "recyclable tasks" in the classroom. When a recyclable task occurs, the teacher first announces the task and identifies the population of people who are to respond:

Initiation	Reply	Evaluation
3:41 T: What else, what else Edward, what do you think we could put there that starts with an *M?*	Carolyn: (raises hand)	
3:42 T: Somebody in your family, Edward.	E: (shrugs shoulders no)	

Then on successive turns of eliciting, the teacher only announces the students who are to reply, but does not mention the task:

Initiation	Reply	Evaluation
3:43 T: All right, Jerome.	Audrey: I know, I know. (raises hand)	

Initiation	Reply	Evaluation
3:44 T: What?	Audrey: Man.	T: Man, good for you, Audrey, that's a very good one for here. Very good.
3:45 T: Ernesto?	E: I know, I know.	
	E: Markel, Markel.	T: Margaret?
	E: Markel (or Martha).	T: Markel, that's a good word for here.
3:46 T: Jerome.	J: My name starts with an *M*, like you know Pittman, P-I-T-T-M-A-N. Man.	
		T: The man part, that's right. You've got the word man at the end of your name.
	Jeannie: (raises hand)	
3:47 T: Jeannie?	J: (pause) I had it and I lost it.	T: Uh, ya.

Griffin and Humphrey say that the work of identifying the students on successive turns makes it unnecessary to restate the task each time.

With the basic individual nomination procedure, both the task and the population of people who are to respond are identified explicitly. In recyclables, the respondent is mentioned repeatedly, while the task is mentioned only at the outset. In another variation of this procedure, automatic turn-allocation procedures (Griffin and Humphrey, 1978), neither the task nor the respondent population is explicitly stated. Task identification and turn-allocation are accomplished by the materials employed in the lesson. Automatic turn-allocation occurs regularly in reading groups (McDermott, 1976; Griffin and Humphrey, 1978). Here, the teacher does not overtly assign the floor to a student at every turn. Instead, turns are predetermined at the outset of the activity, as when the teacher announces that each member of the reading group will read one paragraph. On such occasions, Griffin (personal communication) says it is as if the white spaces in between the printed paragraphs, not the teacher, do the work of fixing turns.

Floor holding by nonverbal means, recyclable tasks, and automatic turn-allocation are examples of emergent conventions in the classrooms. A convention, according to Lewis (1969), is a regularity in the behavior of members of a community based on the expectation that everyone else will conform to the regularity. These conventions are emergent because they are built up over the course of interaction between teachers and students; they are not contracts signed and agreed upon at the beginning of a school year.

Invitations to bid. The teacher also asked students to raise their hands as part of an elicitation act:

Initiation	Reply	Evaluation
3:8 T: . . . raise your hand. Whose name any children, whose name begins with letter (pointing to the letter S)?	J: (raises hand)	

Initiation	Reply	Evaluation
3:9 T: Jerome.	J: Sabrina.	T: Sabrina, Sabrina.
4:70 T: Raise your hand if you know where Leola's house would go on this map.	Many: (raise hands)	
4:71 T: Edward, where do you think Leola's house would go? Come, come and see and we'll see if any of the other people would agree with you.	E: (points to map)	T: Edward says over here.

In this typical example, many students raised their hands in response to the teacher's invitation. The teacher then selected one respondent from those who had raised their hands. Thus, the instruction "raise your hand" invites the students to bid for the floor. The respondent is then selected from the population of bidders.

The teacher invited the students to bid for the floor in other, less explicit ways as well. The teacher initiated elicitations with a variety of the expression, "Who knows the answer?" This type of elicitation, like the more obvious "raise your hand," asks students to make themselves known to the teacher.

Hand raising was the preferred method of bidding for the floor in this classroom. However, on some occasions, students bid for the floor by saying, "I do," "I know," "me, me," by calling "teacher, teacher" or the teacher's name, by finger clicking, or by heavy breathing. Each of these student procedures was successful in gaining access to the floor.

This means of allocating the floor to the next speaker is the invitation to bid turn-allocation procedure. It is shown in figure 3.2.

Note that this turn-taking procedure goes across two teacher-student exchanges. During the first exchange, the teacher invites the pupils to bid, and the pupils do so. During the second exchange, the teacher nominates pupils, and they reply. The teacher then evaluates the content of the students' replies.

Invitations to reply. A third respondent-selection procedure enables students to state what they know directly. When this turn-allocation procedure is in use, students reply, often in unison, without being named or obtaining the floor by bidding. This invitation to reply turn-allocation procedure is realized by a sentence completion form, a chorus elicitation form (compare Mehan, 1974a), and a *wh* question form.

In chapter 2 I described the teacher's practice of beginning an elicitation utterance and then pausing. Students completed the sentence begun by the teacher:

Initiation	Reply	Evaluation
5:13 T: I called the tractor a "mm . . ."	R: Machine.	T: Machine, Rafael good, I called it a machine.
5:18 T: See the . . .	J: Street.	T: Street, good, "see the street."
5:33 T: But then it says "see the . . ."	__: Cafeteria.	

This sentence completion elecitation procedure serves a respondent-selection function as well as an information-exchange function. It permits students to answer in unison without specifically being nominated as next speaker.

FIGURE 3.2. THE INVITATION TO BID
TURN-ALLOCATION PROCEDURE.

Initiation	Reply	Evaluation

T: Elicits + invites
        bids
    └──────────────┘   Many: Bid   C ────[+] Accepts

T: (Elicits + names
        Child A   Child A: Replies   [+] Prompts
    └──────────────┘   I

                                                                 $\begin{bmatrix} + \\ \emptyset \end{bmatrix}$ Rejects

Key: C = correct reply; I = incorrect reply; $\emptyset$ = no evaluation.

Chorus elicitations also explicitly invite students to answer in unison:

Initiation	Reply	Evaluation
4:46 T: And last of all, anybody, whose name is this? (raises card)	Many: Victor.	
	E: Everett.	T: Everett, yes, it's your name. Well, I see we'll have to do a lot more names so that you can learn to read them and pass out books with people's names on them, and papers with people's names on them, and things like that.
5:7 T: Let's hear some of		

Initiation	Reply	Evaluation
the rest of you.	Many: The map.	T: The map, ok.
5:23 T: Let's try it again.	All: This is a map.	T: Good.

Students are also invited to reply directly when the teacher elicits information using a *wh* question form. The following are representative examples:

Initiation	Reply	Evaluation
3:6 T: What is this, an M?	Many: S and M.	T: See like a snake.
4:8 T: What does it say?	C: Alberto.	T: Alberto, Alberto, all right.
4:45 T: Um, whose name is this?	L: Mercedes.	T: Mercedes, all right.
5:10 T: Well, is it a school? What is this?	Many: Map.	T: It's a map, that's right, and this says map too.

The invitation to reply turn-allocation procedure is shown in figure 3.3.

In each initiation act, the teacher not only directs, informs, or elicits information from the students, she also identifies the population of students who are to reply. The next

FIGURE 3.3. THE INVITATION TO REPLY
TURN-ALLOCATION PROCEDURE.

Initiation	Reply	Evaluation

C————[+] Accepts

T: Elicits + invites
   replies   Many: Reply   [+] Rejects

I $\begin{bmatrix} + \\ \emptyset \end{bmatrix}$ Prompts

Key: C = correct reply; I = incorrect reply; $\emptyset$ = no evaluation.

speaker is selected by one of three procedures: individual nomination, invitations to bid, or by invitations to reply. The individual nomination turn-allocation procedure identifies the next respondent by name. The invitation to bid procedure selects the next speaker from those who have bid for the floor. The invitation to reply procedure allows a group of pupils to respond directly without first being awarded the floor. As table 3.1 shows, this interactional work is visible in virtually every speech act initiated by the teacher.

These three procedures for specifying the next speaker constitute the basic turn-allocation apparatus of this classroom. These procedures are interactional, in that their completion is a joint production, with contributions by teacher and students. In order for interaction in these lessons to proceed smoothly, a turn allocated by the teacher must be taken by a student or students. Just as a compelling speaker requires an attentive listener (Erickson and Shultz, 1978), successful turn allocation requires complementary turn taking. The teacher employs these procedures to help insure that academic instruction is conducted in an orderly manner.

Revealing the Basic Turn-Allocation Apparatus of Classroom Lessons

Three techniques by which the teacher allocated turns to students during lessons have been located: individual nominations, invitations to bid, and invitations to reply. Most

TABLE 3.1. THE DISTRIBUTION OF
TURN-ALLOCATION PROCEDURES.

Teacher's speech acts	Turn-allocation procedure				
	Individual nomination	Invitation to bid	Invitation to reply	Other	Total
Directive	22	0	6	0	28
Informative	12	0	75	0	89
Choice elicitation	37	3	21	0	61
Product elicitation	137	37	105	2	279
Process elicitation	11	1	3	0	15
Metaprocess elicitation	8	0	0	0	8
Total	227	41	210	2	480

teacher-student interaction in these lessons was organized by these procedures. A goal of this research was to insure that these procedures were oriented to the participants, and were not just a researcher's analytic device. Therefore I examined the actions of teachers and students themselves for the purpose of seeing whether the machinery I described actually organized the behavior of the participants during the course of their interaction.

This methodological procedure was employed because the methods that participants in an event use to accomplish routine forms of interaction are hard to see under normal circumstances (Garfinkel, 1967; Mehan and Wood, 1975:98, 107, 113-114). But this interactional work does become visible when normal circumstances are disrupted. In a disruption, people engage in recovery work to reestablish the normal forms of interaction (Goffman, 1961:45ff; Garfinkel, 1967). This recovery work displays and informs what is normally hidden from view, namely the interactional work that accomplishes normal forms of interaction.

There is a precedent for using this strategy to reveal the

interactional work organizing interaction in classrooms available in the study of everyday interaction. Durkheim (1896) recommended studying deviations from normality as a way of seeing social organization under normal circumstances. Garfinkel (1967), playing on this point, first proposed "breaching studies" to reveal the interactional activities that constitute normal scenes under normal circumstances. He instructed students to disrupt normal interactional patterns in stores, homes, restaurants, under the assumption that work employed to recover a sense of normality would inform an understanding of the work employed to sustain normality under normal conditions. These demonstrations produced a severe strain on participants, and they were abandoned as unethical.

Subsequent work has attempted to reveal the interactional activities sustaining a sense of social order without disrupting participants' personal lives. Garfinkel and others (see Mehan and Wood, 1975) have proposed "self-breaching studies" to reveal one's taken-for-granted interactional practices. Wearing inverted lenses, listening to auditory allusions and side tone delay mechanisms, and doing Zato coding are some suggested self-breaching procedures. Shumsky and Mehan (1974) have devised "ethnographic variations" of naturally occurring events to reveal the interactional work that sustains a sense of social order. Participants in a naturally occurring event are denied access to some of the taken-for-granted features in a modified scene. The interactional work that assembled the naturally occurring scene becomes visible in the contrast between it and the modified scene.

Ramos (1973a, 1973b) recommends looking at these situations in which people naturally cause trouble for each other, rather than having researchers artificially disrupt others' lives. A variety of this strategy has been adopted here.

In general interaction, if an expected event does not occur, people account for its absence (Garfinkel, 1967). If a person does not reply when spoken to, for example, others are likely to provide accounts like "he didn't hear me," "he must be upset," and the like (Schegloff, 1972:1086-1087;

Mehan and Wood, 1975:132-134). This notion of accounting for absences, derived from the study of everyday interaction, was applied to this analysis of classroom interaction to determine if the turn-allocation apparatus described guided classroom participants.

There is an obligatory co-occurrence relationship between initiator and respondent in each of the three procedures for allocating turns in lessons. The respondent identified in the initiation frame has the right to the floor in the next reply frame. When this co-occurrence relationship is maintained, a symmetry between initiator and respondent is established and turn taking proceeds smoothly. Therefore, it seemed reasonable to assume that if this symmetry was broken the participants would react to the absence of the co-occurrence relationship. More specifically, if an expected turn-taking co-occurrence relationship was not maintained across initiation and reply frames, then the participants would mark the violation in some way, and work to reestablish the symmetry of the co-occurrence relationship.

Thus, the general method of verification was to propose that certain reply acts would occur with certain initiation acts. For example, a speaker allocated the floor in the initiation act would be the next respondent; a request for bids for the floor would be followed by bids. To determine if this co-occurrence relationship structured teacher-student exchanges, a potential first entry in a turn-allocation sequence was located. The next entry in the sequence was then predicted. If the prediction held, this sequence was catalogued as an instance of a normal form of interaction. If the prediction did not hold, what the participants did in the absence of the predicted relationship became the focus of study. The application of this general procedure to the specific turn-allocation procedures will now be described.

The individual nomination procedure governing access to the floor specifies that the student named by the teacher has the right to reply next. But what if a student other than the one nominated speaks instead?

The transcripts of three such instances appear below.

Initiation	Reply	Evaluation
4:15 T: Edward, do you think you know who this is? (holding up a name-card)	C: (with hand raised) I do.	T: Wait a minute.

Initiation	Reply	Evaluation
4:54 T: (indicating a map of the schoolyard hung on the wall of the room) Alberto, what were you going to put down here? // Jerome: Yesterday.	A: Truck. C: A tractor.	T: The truck, yeah.
4:55 T: We still need to do that, don't we? What color was it?	C: Yellow. A: Yellow.	T: Wait a minute, let Alberto say it since he's going to make it. T: Yellow, that's right.

Initiation	Reply	Evaluation
8:111 T: Where, where		

Initiation	Reply	Evaluation
were your parents born?	R: San Diego.	
	E: Tijuana.	
8:112 W: Where was you born?		T: People we can't hear Roberto.
		__: Shh, shh.
	E: San Diego.	C: Shh!
8:113 T: Your Parents were . . .	E: San Diego.	T: Edward.
		C: Why don't you guys shut up?
		P: Let him talk, you guys talked already.
		C: It's his turn now.
		T: It is, it's Roberto's turn, Edward.

In each of these cases, a student replied when the floor had been awarded to another student. In the first two cases, the teacher reprimanded the student who interrupted. In the last case (8:111-113), both the teacher and the students reprimanded the student who interrupted.

The invitation to bid procedure specifies that students who think they know the reply to a teacher's elicitation are supposed to bid for the floor. The teacher then nominates a next speaker from those who bid. That speaker is supposed to reply to the elicitation. But what if a student replies instead of bidding for the floor? The transcripts of three such instances appear below.

Initiation	Reply	Evaluation
3:15 T: Now, what can you think, can you think of some-thing to eat?	Many: Snakes.	T: Wait a minute, wait a minute.
	Many: (raise hands) Snakes.	T: Wait a minute, raise your hand. Raise your hand. Give people a chance to think.
4:36 T: Uh, whose name // J: Sabrina. T: (raises card)	//C: Sabrina.	T: Raise your hand, raise your hand to give other people a chance to read.
4:93 T: Um, who can think of some words? (draws on board)	Many: Jelly, Jerome.	T: Martin, raise your hand to give other people a chance to think. That's why I want you to raise your hand to give other people a chance to think.

In each of these cases, the teacher invited the student to bid for the floor. When the students replied instead of bidding, they were negatively evaluated.

These actions by the students were negatively evaluated

by the teacher. This evaluative activity marks the absence of the expected form of interaction. She does so in a number of ways: (1) She reprimands them ("wait a minute," 3:15, 4:15, 4:55), marking these instances as violations of turn-taking rules. (2) She describes the proper way to gain the floor under the invitation to bid rule ("raise your hand," 3:15, 4:36, 4:93). (3) She explains the grounds for forbidding the activity ("let Alberto say it since he's going to make it," 4:55; "give other people a chance to think," 3:15, 4:93; "give other people a chance to read," 4:36).

In addition to pointing out inappropriate ways of acting, the teacher's evaluative activity indicates the form that turn taking should take under normal circumstances. When the co-occurrence relationship between speaker and respondent is violated, the teacher engages in interactional work to repair the breach and reestablish the normal form of interaction.

Classroom turn-taking rules, like other normative rules, are tacit (Garfinkel, 1967; Cicourel, 1973). They are seldom formulated, listed, or stated in so many words. When interviewed, participants provide only idealized versions of procedures. The rules for normal operation can be made visible, however, by specifying the conditions that constitute their violation. Rule violations, in turn, can be located by looking for action that participants take in the absence of the expected forms of interaction.

In general interaction, when people account for the absence of expected forms of action, the normally unavailable presence of rules is made visible. Looking to a place of trouble and observing the recovery work being done there to reestablish normal operations reveals the interactional activity that supports the normative order of classroom lessons under normal circumstances.

In summary, teacher-student exchanges in which the respondents identified by the initiator of the speech act respond in the reply frame and receive the appropriate evaluation constitute normal or routine forms of interaction according to the turn-allocation system of this classroom. Exchanges in which participants mark the violation of respondent-selection co-occurrence relationships constitute "sanctioned violations" of this turn-allocation system. (In this book I follow the practice, accepted by many sociologists, of using the verb "sanction" to mean "evaluate negatively." A teacher sanctions a student in response to the form, not the content, of the student's answer.)

A diagram of normal forms and sanctioned violations is displayed in figure 3.4. Normal forms and sanctioned violations are the basic interactional procedures that the teacher employed to complete her practical classroom project of accomplishing academic instruction in an orderly manner. Normal forms are displayed in 88.0 percent of the 480 teacher-initiated exchanges that make up our corpus of materials. Sanctioned violations comprise 5.8 percent. The remaining 6.1 percent are exchanges that diverge from these routine patterns of interaction. Their organization is discussed in the following section.

Achieving Order under Unusual Classroom Circumstances

Under normal classroom circumstances, the teacher operates a turn-allocation apparatus that includes individual nomination, invitation to bid, and invitation to reply turn-allocation procedures in order to instruct students in an orderly manner. But this basic organization is not always maintained. The practical circumstances of the classroom intervene in the basic turn-allocation process during lessons. Students interrupt, lose interest, fail to reply when called on, become distracted by unexpected visitors. These practical circumstances contribute to teacher-student exchanges that diverge from the routine patterns of interaction.

Teacher-student exchanges that diverge from routine patterns of interaction include (1) exchanges in which the respondent-selection co-occurrence relationships are violated but the teacher does not sanction the violation; and (2) exchanges in which the teacher applies a sanction to a seemingly appropriate (normal) behavior.

The relationship between student action and subsequent evaluation produces a typology of interaction. When students' action is appropriate in terms of the basic turn-alloca-

FIGURE 3.4. NORMAL FORMS AND SANCTIONED VIOLATIONS OF THE BASIC TURN-ALLOCATION PROCEDURES.

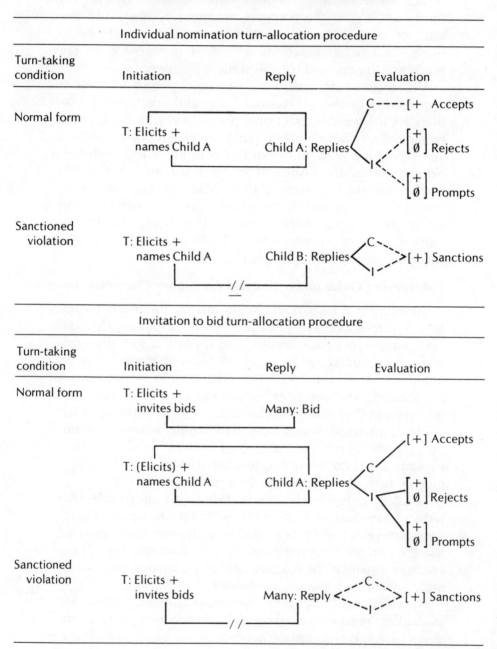

Invitation to reply turn-allocation procedure

Turn-taking condition	Initiation	Reply	Evaluation
Normal form	T: Elicits + invites replies	Students: Reply	C — [+] Accepts I — [+] Rejects or [Ø] prompts
Sanctioned violation	T: Elicits + invites replies	Students: Reply	C, I >[+] Sanctions

Key: Braces indicate co-occurrence relationships; / / indicates a broken co-occurrence relationship; C = correct reply; I = incorrect reply; Ø = no evaluation.

tion procedures and the teacher evaluates students' replies as predicted by the analysis, normal forms of interaction result. When students' action is inappropriate in terms of the turn-allocation system and the teacher negatively evaluates these actions, "sanctioned violations" occur. "Unwarranted sanctions" result when students' actions seem to be appropriate, yet sanctions are applied. When students' actions seem to violate procedures, yet no sanctions are applied, "unsanctioned violations" occur. These interrelationships and the frequency of their occurrence are summarized in table 3.2.

However, "unsanctioned violations" and "unwarranted sanctions" are unacceptable designations. They suggest that interaction in lessons is random and haphazard. Furthermore, they imply that behavior defined as deviant by an observer is not treated as such by the participants themselves. Such a disparity is fatal for theories attempting to account for rule violations (Pollner, 1975).

When action takes place that seems to violate rules, but participants do not mark the violations, it means that the data has not been described adequately. One possible reason for these unsanctioned violations and unwarranted sanctions

TABLE 3.2. TEACHER-STUDENT INTERACTION TYPES AND FREQUENCIES (TOTAL NUMBER OF INTERACTIONS = 480).

	Teacher evaluation					
	Applied as predicted			Not applied as predicted		
Student action	Type	Number	%	Type	Number	%
Appropriate	normal forms of interaction	423	88.1	unwarranted sanctions	2	0.6
Inappropriate	sanctioned violations	28	5.8	unsanctioned violations	27	5.5
Total		451			29	

is that the normative order of the classroom has broken down. Another possibility is that an as yet unspecified system of organization is operating on these occasions. Inasmuch as classroom interaction does not halt at these moments, the latter possibility seems the more plausible.

Since this turn-allocation model does not adequately describe the structuring of the entire organization of the lessons in this corpus, further analysis is necessary. Ideally, the analysis should continue until the organization of all of these anomalous cases is discovered. Viewed in this way, the practical project for the remainder of this chapter is to replace the suspect designations of unsanctioned violations and unwarranted sanctions with designations that provide a more adequate description of the procedures that assemble the organized character of these classroom lessons. Unsanctioned violations and unwarranted sanctions then, are not final explanatory terms; they are provisional designations which serve as flags to warn us that the analysis is not yet complete.

As stated in chapter 1, a goal of this research is to confine the analysis to the interaction, locating the description of the procedures employed to maintain the social organization of lessons in the behavior of participants. This means that attributions to personality characteristics, motivational states, or other mentalisms are avoided, and sociological abstractions like social class, stratification, and the like are not employed unless the influence of such conceptions can be located in the behavior and talk of the participants.

In general, the procedure is to employ context in controlled and measured ways in order to assemble a more complete model of the structuring of classroom lessons. This procedure involves examining the context surrounding anomalous cases in ever increasing increments until the interactional work that organizes classroom lessons when the basic turn-allocation procedures do not operate is located.

More specifically, the analysis of anomalous cases starts with an examination of the co-occurrence relationships between initiation and reply acts. Here, the timing and content of replies are examined to see if these features influence the teacher's acceptance of students' replies that are out of turn. If this additional information provides an adequate account of the anomalous case, the analysis stops. If, however, that additional piece of context is insufficient, slightly more of the context surrounding unsanctioned violations and unwarranted sanctions is brought into focus until their organization can be accounted for. At such times, the phases and progress of the lessons in which unsanctioned violations occur are compared with normal forms and sanctioned violations to see where anomalous cases occur in lessons.

Thus, it should be clear that this procedure does not deny the importance of context in the operation of the basic turn-allocation procedures. Indeed, it isolates the specific aspects of context that influence the operation of both the basic and the improvised turn-allocation methods.

For the purposes of this phase of the analysis, the corpus of twenty-nine anomalous cases was divided according to the turn-allocation procedure employed by the teacher in the initial initiation act of the sequence. There are twenty individual nominations, five invitations to bid, and four invitations to reply in this initial group.

IMPROVISATIONAL STRATEGIES All classroom participants, but especially the teacher, respond to these problematic occurrences. The teacher employs strategies to deal with trouble in the basic machinery used to achieve classroom order. She works to restore order, to go on with the lesson, to complete her agenda of academic objectives.

The teacher adopted several strategies for dealing with violations of the individual nomination procedures. I call these strategies (1) the work of doing nothing, (2) getting through, (3) accepting the unexpected, and (4) opening the floor. The teacher also employed the strategy of doing nothing to handle violations of the invitation to bid and invitation to reply procedures. These strategies account for twenty-one of twenty-nine, or 72 percent, of the anomalous cases.

Combining the results of this analysis of improvisational strategies with the analysis of basic turn-allocation procedures accounts for 472 of 480, or 98.3 percent, of the teacher-initiated sequences. Of the remaining 8 instances, 4 could not be analyzed within the limit of an interactional analysis, and the final 4 could not be analyzed at all, for technical reasons.[1]

This context analysis produces an array of teacher's strategies for coping with trouble in the basic turn-allocation apparatus used to achieve social order in classroom lessons. These improvisational strategies, when coupled with the basic turn-allocation procedures, constitute the machinery that structures the organization of lessons.

The description of the teacher's improvisational strategies begins with those employed when the individual nomination turn-allocation procedure was violated.

The work of doing nothing. In many violations of the individual nomination turn-allocation procedure, students not nominated by the teacher replied before the nominated student. The following example is representative of the five instances in this group of unsanctioned violations (see also 4:136, 4:114, 7:7, and 9:70).

When the teacher asked a student to identify the beginning letter of a word, the following sequence of interaction took place:

Initiation	Reply	Evaluation
4:103 T: Um, Patricia, um jelly, does jelly		

Initiation	Reply	Evaluation
begin like Sabrina or like Jerome? (touches board) Jelly.	P: (no response) J: Jerome.	
4:104 T: Alberto, which does it begin like? Does jelly begin like, does jelly begin like Jerome or Sabrina?	A: (no response)	

The floor was allocated to Patricia by the individual nomination procedure, but Jerome replied before she did. Although Jerome violated the turn-allocation procedure that was in effect, the teacher did not provide an overt verbal sanction. Although Jerome's reply was correct, the teacher did not positively evaluate it. Instead, she ignored Jerome's reply completely, and directed the same elicitation act to another student. The teacher adopted a similar strategy when other students spoke *after* a nominated student spoke, but before the teacher regained possession of the floor (see 4:54, 4:99, 8:111). For example, during the Map lesson, the teacher asked Alberto to indicate what he was going to draw on the map.

Initiation	Reply	Evaluation

4:54
  T: Alberto, what were you going to put down here
  //J: Yesterday.
	A: Truck.
	
	C: A tractor.
		T: The truck, yeah.

Alberto was awarded a turn by the individual nomination procedure. After he replied, but before the teacher spoke again, another student replied. The teacher then praised the reply of the nominated student, but evaluated neither the form nor the content of the interrupting student's reply.

Each of the five replies that came before the nominated students' replies was factually correct; each of the three replies that came after the nominated students' replies was factually incorrect. The teacher's strategy for dealing with all eight of these out-of-turn sequences was to do nothing. She neither evaluated the content of the reply nor sanctioned the poor form. She simply proceeded to the next item on her agenda.

The teacher adopted a similar strategy for dealing with violations of invitation to bid and invitation to reply procedures. When the teacher asked students to suggest words that start with *J* during a reading preparedness lesson, the following exchange with Sabrina took place:

Initiation	Reply	Evaluation
4:94 T: Um, who can think of some words, some things, some names that start with this sound "J, J, JJ." (touches *J* on board)	S: (raises hand) S: J. C: (lowers hand)	
4:95 T: Ah, Mercedes.	M: June. Many: (raise hands) ———	T: June? All right. T: Wait a minute, wait a minute.

Since the teacher employed the invitation to bid procedure, students were to bid for the floor. Sabrina, however, bid, and in the same turn of talk, replied. Her reply was both incorrect and out of turn. The teacher neither commented on the incorrect reply nor evaluated its improper form; instead, she called on another student. [2]

Doing nothing in the face of violations of classroom procedures does evaluative work. Ignoring talk taken out of turn functions as a "mild sanction." The co-occurrence relationship tying initiation, reply, and evaluation acts (see chapter 2) dictates that a positive evaluation follows a correct reply. Responding to the correct content of the students' replies when they are out of turn, the teacher refuses to incorporate the students' replies into the lesson. By doing nothing, the teacher is telling the students that their replies are not acceptable in this form even though they may be factually correct.

This teacher's strategy has practical consequences. If the teacher reacted overtly to all deviations from normality, she would only be doing "police work." The work of doing nothing, then, retains the teacher's control of the lesson format in subtle ways. It enables the teacher to complete her projects without constantly sanctioning violations of classroom rules in an overt manner.

A prototypical example of the "work of doing nothing" is visually represented in figure 3.5.

Getting through. Sometimes during the course of a lesson, the teacher has difficulty in eliciting the information she wants from the students. She invites bids for the floor, but receives none. She calls on particular students by name, only to have them turn away. She opens the floor to direct replies, only to be faced by silence.

At such times, the delicate thread of order running through lessons is in danger of breaking. A constant fear expressed by teachers is "losing the lesson," having students' attention wander, with the lesson ending in disarray. When this basic item on teachers' agendas is in jeopardy, they often ignore the more refined aspects of classroom decorum. They allow deviations from classroom procedures to pass until they can

FIGURE 3.5. THE WORK OF DOING NOTHING.

Turn-allocation procedure	Initiation	Reply	Evaluation
Individual nomination	T: Elicits + names Child A	Child B: Replies: C	T: Ø
		Child A: Replies: C	T: Accepts
	T: Elicits + names Child A	Child A: Replies: C	T: Accepts
		Child B: Replies: I	T: Ø
Invitation to bid	T: Elicits + invites bids	Child A: Replies: I	T: Ø
Invitation to reply	T: Elicits //	Child A: Replies	
		Child B: Replies	
		Child C: Replies	T: Accepts

Key: C = correct reply; I = incorrect reply; Ø = no evaluation.

"get through the rough spots," and "get the lesson moving again."

Two examples of the teacher's strategy of "getting through" occur in the Map Words lesson. In one sense, this lesson was continually plagued with difficulty. This was the first time that the teacher had engaged the students in a responsive reading lesson. The students were having difficulty identifying the words printed on a large storyboard in front of them. The teacher prompted virtually all replies offered by the students.

One particularly difficult spot was when the teacher asked the students to read the line of the story that said "see room 24."

Initiation	Reply	Evaluation
5:26 T: (points to second		

Initiation	Reply	Evaluation
line of the story).	All: See . . .	
5:27 T: "See . . . " Everett, you figured this one out before, "see . . . "	E: 24.	
5:28 T: What 24?	Alberto: Room 24.	
	Many: 24.	T: Good, Alberto, "see room 24."

The teacher pointed to the line in the story that she wanted the students to read (5:26). The students produced only the first word in the line. She repeated the first word again (5:27), but was not accompanied by the students. Unsuccessful in having the students reply in unison, she called on Everett to reply alone. Everett provided another of the words in the line (5:27). The teacher then encouraged him to provide the missing word "room." The teacher had oriented her body toward Everett and was maintaining eye contact with him. In so doing, she was nominating Everett to be the next speaker by nonverbal means. Before Everett replied, Alberto and then many other students replied with the complete correct reply the teacher had been working for. Even though this reply technically violated the individual nomination turn-allocation procedure, the teacher did not sanction it as a violation. Indeed, she praised Alberto for supplying the much-sought-after reply.

The teacher found herself in similar circumstances later in this same lesson. She had written five words on flash cards for the students to identify. At one point, she held up the card that read "cafeteria."

Initiation	Reply	Evaluation
5:77 T: Now who knows		

Initiation	Reply	Evaluation
what this one says (holds up new card). This is the long word. Who knows what it says?	A: Cafeteria.	T: Cafeteria, Audrey, good for you.

Her first request for students to bid for the floor was unproductive. The teacher provided a clue, "This is the long word." Still no response. She repeated the invitation to bid, "Who knows what it says?" After a considerable pause, Audrey supplied the correct reply. As with the previous example (5:27-28), even though this reply technically violated the turn-taking procedures—even though the student replied without bidding for the floor—it was warmly received.

It seems that when the teacher is having trouble with the lesson, and students give her a good answer but violate classroom procedure to do so, she lets the rule violation pass in the interest of getting through the difficulty.

Opening the floor. In three instances of unsanctioned violations of individual nomination procedures, a student not allocated the floor replied correctly after a nominated student either declined a turn or replied incorrectly.

During the course of reading the book about Martin Luther King's childhood, questions about various people's ages relative to King's assassination came up in conversation. Wallace was particularly interested in the teacher's age at the time of King's death (9:70). The teacher asked Wallace to compute her age at that time. When he arrived at the answer, he signaled the teacher. The teacher interrupted reading the story to allocate the floor to Wallace by the individual nomination procedure:

Initiation	Reply	Evaluation
9:79 T: (nods to Wallace)	W: You were 41.	

Initiation	Reply	Evaluation
	(lowers hand)	T: Uh, 49, take away 7, pretty close.
	G: 42.	T: Yeah, 42 is right Greg.

Wallace replied, but his reply was factually incorrect. The teacher prompted this reply, and Greg followed the teacher's evaluation with the correct information. The individual nomination turn-allocation procedure I have described to this point implies that the child who replies without nomination will be reprimanded. However, in this case Greg was not sanctioned. Instead, the teacher positively evaluated his reply.

At one point in the Birthplaces lesson, the teacher selected Wallace by the individual nomination procedure to locate the state of Virginia on the map. After he did so, the teacher directed a metaprocess elicitation to him.

Initiation	Reply	Evaluation
8:132 T: Virginia, can you find it?	W: (goes to board and points)	
8:133 T: How'd you know that?	W: I don't know.	
	C: Cause it's a V.	T: I think cause it's probably cause it's a V. (pins on map)

Wallace declined his turn. Immediately thereafter, Carolyn provided a possible way by which Wallace's answer could have been obtained. The individual nomination procedure implies that a student who replies when the floor has been awarded to another is negatively evaluated. However, in this case when Carolyn spoke out of turn her response was positively evaluated by the teacher.

These three interactional sequences in the initial corpus of unsanctioned violations of turn-taking rules have identical characteristics. In each case, the reply by the student who was not allocated the floor came after the nominated student had access to his or her allocated turn and before the teacher initiated a new elicitation act. In 9:79 (see also 8:125), the reply by the unnominated student came after the nominated student had replied incorrectly. In 8:132, the out-of-turn reply came after the nominated student had declined his turn. In all cases, the reply by the unnominated student was correct and supplied information sought by the teacher.

The presence of this recurrent pattern suggests that after a nominated student replies incorrectly, or declines a turn, the floor is open once again. Other students can reply directly before the teacher takes the floor back for reallocation. This state of affairs is not so much turn *allocation* by the teacher as it is turn *taking* by the students.

Such segments of interaction impressively demonstrate that classroom lessons are collaborative enterprises. Both teachers and students cooperatively accomplish opening the floor. When the teacher nominates a student and that student does not complete the turn, other students actively create response opportunities for themselves. The teacher accepts this creativity.

The strategy of "opening the floor" is schematically represented in figure 3.6.

Accepting the unexpected. Students often surprise teachers. Unfortunately for teachers, sometimes students produce less than expected. Pleasantly for teachers, students also sometimes provide more than expected. Just as teachers temporarily suspend basic classroom rules in order to get through the unpleasant unexpected moments, so too they temporarily suspend classroom rules when surprised by pleasant unexpected behavior.

There are three such instances in the initial corpus of unsanctioned violations of the individual nomination turn-allocation rules. One of these will be described (see also 9:3 and 9:44).

FIGURE 3.6. THE IMPROVISATIONAL STRATEGY OF
OPENING THE FLOOR.

Turn-allocation procedure	Initiation	Reply	Evaluation
Individual nomination	T: Elicits + names Child A	Child A: < Ø / I	
		Child B: Replies: C	T: Accepts

Key: C = correct reply; I = incorrect reply; Ø = no reply.

During the *S* and *J* Words reading preparedness lesson, the teacher asked Veronica to tell her about the beginning letter of the word "sandwich":

Initiation	Reply	Evaluation
4:101 J: I didn't know it was supposed to have a cross on top.		
4:102 T: I want you to tell me whether it begins like Jerome or like Sabrina. Um, let's see, uh Veronica, "sandwich"—does sandwich begin like Sabrina or like Jerome?	__: Neither.	
	V: Like Sabrina.	T: Good.
	J: Sandwich, yeah, cuz it's got an *n* in it.	T: That's right.

Although the floor was allocated to Veronica by individual nomination, many other students replied. The teacher employed the strategy of doing nothing to treat this deviation from normal classroom procedure. Then Veronica answered correctly. After the teacher accepted this reply, but before she could move to the next item on her agenda, Jerome replied. Although his reply was out of turn, the teacher praised it.

The content of this reply is informative for understanding this seeming deviation from normal procedure. Jerome's was a particularly good reply. He provided a metaprocess reply when only a product reply was called for. Replies that provide more than expected, like those which provide less than expected, produce an asymetrical co-occurrence relationship. Replies that provide more than expected, unlike those which produce less than expected, are allowed to pass even if they violate basic turn-allocation procedures.

This analysis suggests that accepting unexpectedly good answers is a strategic manipulation of the tacit rule system that governs the organization of respondent selection in these lessons. This strategy functions to assist the teacher's progress through the substance of her lesson agenda. Perhaps more importantly, this strategy also functions to provide opportunities for "special" or "extra" participation.

The teacher's strategy of accepting the unexpected is displayed in figure 3.7.

THE BOUNDARIES OF CONTEXTUAL ANALYSIS To this point, "the work of doing nothing," "getting through,"

FIGURE 3.7. THE IMPROVISATIONAL STRATEGY OF ACCEPTING THE UNEXPECTED.

Initiation	Reply	Evaluation
T: Elicits + names product Child A	Child A: Replies: C	
	Child B: Replies: metaprocess reply	T: Accepts

"opening the floor," and "accepting the unexpected," strategies that the teacher employed to deal with disruptions in the basic system for organizing classroom lessons have been examined. These strategies were located by examining the context surrounding so-called unsanctioned violations of turn-allocation procedures in increasing increments. The features that characterize these strategies were located in the interaction between participants. Their description was made without recourse to psychological attributions, motivational states, socioeconomic status, or other characteristics of individual participants.

The addition of these strategies to the set of basic turn-allocation procedures provides an adequate description of 72.0 percent of our anomalous cases and 98.3 percent of the total corpus. However, two unsanctioned violations and both unwarranted sanctions remain to be described. These four anomalies cannot be accounted for within the limits of an interactional analysis. To account for their occurrence, it would have been necessary to invoke information about the students' personal characteristics or their presumed relationship to the teacher, or to make appeals to the teacher's motivations, intentions, or psychological predisposition toward the students. Although it is possible to speculate about the influence of such background and dispositional factors, it was not possible to say unequivocally that these factors were operating at the moment in question and still remain faithful to the criteria that explanatory factors be located in the interaction.

For example, in three of the four remaining anomalous cases (3:10, 3:20, 4:97), the teacher seemed to provide response opportunities for certain members of the class to the exclusion of others. While that observation can be grounded interactionally, the basis upon which these distinctions were made can not be grounded equivalently. Speculations about the relative relationships of the students to the teacher could be made to account for these interactional patterns. For example, the student for whom the teacher held the floor was younger, and impressed the classroom observers as being timid and shy. The students whom the teacher "closed down"

appeared to the researchers to be assertive and more sophisticated academically. However, these characterizations of
the students were composites that emerged as the year progressed. There is no evidence that the teacher saw the students in that way in the first week of school and employed
those grounds in the moments in question. Rather than
ground my analysis in such speculations, I prefer to leave the
question open.

As a result of this analysis of anomalous cases, the data
originally displayed in table 3.2 as unsanctioned violations
and unwarranted sanctions can be recast as shown in table
3.3.

This analysis does not deny the existence of motivation,
intentionality, past experiences, ethnicity, socioeconomic
status. Teachers may well be predisposed toward or against
certain students. A teacher's knowledge of students' biographies may well influence the teacher's evaluation of those

TABLE 3.3. TEACHER-STUDENT INTERACTION TYPES AND
FREQUENCIES AFTER REANALYSIS
(TOTAL NUMBER OF INTERACTIONS = 480).

Student action	Teacher evaluation applied as predicted			Unexplained cases	
	Type	Number	%	Number	%
Appropriate[1]	normal forms of interaction basic procedures	423	—	8[2]	—
	improvisational strategies	21	—	—	—
	total normal interactions	444	92.5	—	—
Inappropriate[1]	sanctioned violations	28	5.8	—	—
Total		472	98.3	8	1.7

1. Appropriate or inappropriate according to the turn-allocation procedures.

2. Four of these cases could not be explained for technical reasons;
four could not be explained within the limits of the interactional analysis.

students during lessons. Students from different backgrounds may perform differently in schools.

I am not saying that such factors do not operate in teacher-student interaction or do not affect educational outcomes. I *am* complaining that social science research has, for too long now, appealed to factors like the backgrounds of students, the characteristics of teachers, the quality of schools as input factors when making claims about educational outcomes without showing how these factors actually operate in the day-to-day activities of schooling. This constitutive ethnographic approach is taken in order to limit the use of dispositional properties and background factors as explanatory devices when their influence cannot be located in the interaction.

We need to avoid promiscuous speculation if we are to make well-grounded connections between social interaction and social structure. When the limits of the immediate context have been reached through a constitutive analysis of events, principled reasons are provided for considering the influence of factors that existed prior to and surround the assembly of particular events. On the one hand, increasing the boundaries of the analysis in systematic and controlled ways means classroom events will be placed in the larger context of the society. On the other hand, social structure, past history, school organization will be located in the day-to-day interaction of participants in educational settings. The overall result will be to show the ways in which social interaction and social structure ceaselessly inform one another.

Conclusions

The teacher in the classroom adopts a utilitarian position vis-à-vis the sociological problem of social order. She wants her classroom to be orderly so that her academic objectives can be achieved systematically.

Under normal classroom circumstances, the teacher in this classroom operated a turn-allocation apparatus, which included the individual nomination, invitation to bid, and invitation to reply turn-allocation procedures to facilitate orderly instruction.

This basic organization of lessons was not always maintained, because practical circumstances intruded upon the turn-allocation process. These practical circumstances dictated that the teacher also have methods for achieving academic objectives that were responsive to spontaneous, unexpected, and emergent occurrences. Those techniques that the teacher used to facilitate her lesson objectives when practical circumstances intervened were called improvisational strategies. Included in this repertoire of improvisational strategies are the work of doing nothing, opening the floor, getting through, and accepting the unexpected.

The participants' orientation to this interactional apparatus was determined by the action they took in the absence of expected forms of interaction. Classroom participants accounted for the absence of predicted co-occurrence relationships between initiator and respondent. They engaged in recovery work to restore the turn-allocation machinery to normal when a co-occurrence relationship that sustained the normative order of lessons was broken. This orientation to the turn-allocation machinery on the part of participants leads to the conclusion that the researcher's model for assembling the social order of lessons is the participants' model as well.

These improvisational strategies, when coupled with the basic turn-allocation procedures, represent the repertoire of procedures by which the teacher organized lessons and distributed participation (Philips, 1974) among students. This repertoire amounts to the interactional mechanism for maintaining social order during classroom lessons.

The interactional activity of classroom participants collaboratively constructs the organization of classroom lessons. Hence, this analysis reveals a way in which the social structure of routine social events is structured by the participants' collaborative work.

STRATEGIC MANIPULATION OF THE TURN-ALLOCATION SYSTEM   The teacher's use of basic turn-allocation procedures was sensitive to contextual particulars. When some students monopolized the use of the invitation to reply form, the teacher shifted to the other respondent-selection techniques. Conversely, the teacher shifted to the invitation to reply format to warm up the class at the beginning of a slow-starting lesson (see for example, CIS #5). The teacher's use of a basic turn-allocation procedure was neither random nor haphazard. Instead, the use of a particular procedure on a particular occasion reflected a strategic relationship between the teacher's academic agenda and the practical classroom situation at the time.

The teacher's use of a particular improvisational strategy was likewise influenced by practical circumstances. The "objective" characteristics of the anomalous sequences were similar. In each case, students violated the turn-taking rules of the lesson. (This similarity is displayed by comparing figures 3.5-3.7, which depict the teacher's strategies for responding to violations of turn-taking procedures, with figures 3.1-3.4, which depict the basic turn-allocation procedures.) However, the content of a student's reply did not exclusively determine a teacher's evaluation of the reply. The content of a student's reply is embedded in a swarm of contextual features. The topic of the lesson (such as initial consonant recognition, responsive reading, word recognition), the phase of a lesson (opening, closing), the course of a lesson (proceeding smoothly, trouble receiving replies), the form and content of a reply, and the student responding, among others, were contextual particulars that contributed to the teacher's moment-to-moment decisions about the use of a strategy for dealing with the unexpected occurrences in lessons.

These strategic manipulations of the normative aspects of the turn-allocation machinery generate differential response opportunities for certain members of the class. The teacher's use of the turn-allocation machinery, then, not only serves to preserve and reestablish the normative character of interaction; it also functions to distribute participation among certain students according to different classroom circumstances. It can also be used to provide the teacher with an effective method for controlling replies from students who have dominated the previous work of interaction, or to facilitate the participation of particularly quiet students.

Thus, the teacher's evaluation of students was not under

the immediate stimulus control of the proceeding student response. The teacher's response was negotiated in each moment of teacher-student interaction.

Because the teacher's decision to accept or reject a student's reply is contextually bound, mechanistic conceptions are inappropriate models for describing interaction in this situation. A mechanistic model would treat the ingredients of action in this turn-taking system (teacher's strategies, students' behavior, the classroom situation), as three analytically separate and discrete entities. The teacher's repertoire would be depicted as a list of strategies selected in advance of lessons. The teacher would be seen as rationally choosing a course of action from that preselected list and matching it automatically to students' behavior in a social situation.

Either an interpretive (Cicourel, 1973) or a mutually constitutive (Mehan and Wood, 1975) model of action seems more appropriate as a metaphor for the teacher's use of strategies from her repertoire. The teacher's strategies are applied within particular practical circumstances, which are not independent of the people and their behavior in it. A particular strategy does not flash in the face of particular behavior in the classroom. The teacher does not automatically match strategies and behavior in the classroom; she interprets students' behavior against a constantly changing background of practical circumstances.

CLASSROOM RULES, THE NORMATIVE ORDER, AND INTERACTIONAL COMPETENCE   The presence of the kind of tacit, normative rule system that has been described in this chapter requires special skills on the part of the participants in the setting. Students must orient their behavior to the procedures for gaining access to the floor in order to appropriately engage in classroom interaction from the point of view of the teacher. If students deviate from this normative system, sanctions are imposed by the teacher, and sometimes by other students.

Therefore, students must engage in interpretive work to analyze the flow of interaction and provide the appropriate behavior. To participate in lessons, students must engage in interpretive work that is equivalent to the work that we did to construct our analysis.

The basic turn-allocation procedures specify competing behavior for different occasions of interaction. On the one hand, when the individual nomination or invitation to bid procedure is in effect, students must wait to be nominated and reply one at a time. On the other hand, when the invitation to reply procedure is in effect, students can reply directly and in unison. To participate in lessons, students must pick up the subtle cues that signal the applicability of a given procedure on a particular occasion of interaction.

The teacher's use of improvisational strategies also imposes significant interpretive problems for students. Since the teacher employs turn-allocation procedures that are sensitive to context, students must be able to interpret the special character of these occurrences. So, while these improvisational strategies manipulate the normative character of interaction in strategic ways for the teacher, they often pose conflicting situations to the students. Students' successful participation in classroom lessons is at least partially determined by their abilities to deal with this conflicting information.

The skills that students use to interpret these tacit classroom rules, and the interactional strategies they use to incorporate their own agenda items into this predominantly teacher-centered machinery, are explored in the following chapter.

4

COMPETENT MEMBERSHIP IN THE CLASSROOM COMMUNITY

A THEORETICAL distinction is often made between socialization and formal education. While socialization is said to be the interactional and symbolic process involved in the transmission of the general skills and abilities that everyone needs to know in order to be a competent member of a society, formal education is said to be concerned with the transmission of specialized skills, logical operations, and abstract systems. Whereas socializing the uninitiated members is said to be the general responsibility of all competent members of society and occurs everywhere, formal education is conducted by specialized agents, namely teachers, at specialized locations, namely schools. The medium of transmission of knowledge is also said to be different in education than in socialization. The general skills and abilities of societal membership are said to be transmitted by demonstration and modeling; the specialized knowledge of formal education is transmitted primarily by verbal instruction.

This theoretical distinction collapses in modern American schools, for socialization as well as education occurs in the classroom. Classrooms are admittedly academic. "They are places where people meet for the purposes of giving and receiving instruction" (Waller, 1932:8). Instruction is also provided in dominant cultural values and conventional morality. "No community or nation really wants, nor can it afford to have its educators really educate, for this would be subversive to the status quo; it wants its youth socialized" (Parsons, 1959). Dreeben (1968), for example, points out that

American classrooms instruct students that working independently, achieving the highest level of success possible, and applying universalistic criteria are cultural values. Competition could easily be added to that list. Parsons (1959) says that in the socialization role the teacher is responsible for emancipating children from their primary emotional attachment to the family, instilling achievement as the mode of differentiation among people, promoting universalistic (familial) norms and values, motivating and training for performance in roles that are beneficial to society, and encouraging conformance to the expectations of others as a technique of social control.

Bernstein (1973) seeks to explain the various dimensions of school culture, and especially to deduce the major consequences that flow from their interrelations. Following Durkheim (1938), he identifies two organically linked behavioral consequences that the school transmits to the pupil. One is the "expressive order." Similar to Durkheim's moral order, the expressive order is the basis of societal integration. It links pupils together in a collectivity. The other is the "instrumental order." This is the body of facts, procedures, practices, and judgments that are needed to acquire specific skills that can be genuinely measured by objective methods. This order is transmitted so as to divide pupils according to ability. Thus the expressive order unites and the instrumental order divides.

These observations suggest that it would be productive to look closely at the interplay of socialization and education in the classroom. That topic will be addressed by investigating the composition of students' interactional competence in the classroom.

Approaches to Competence

Interactional competence is defined here in terms of effective participation or membership in the classroom. This definition is intentionally broad in scope. It is intended to encompass the requisites for communication with others, and the interpretation of language, behavior, rules, and other normative dimensions of classroom life. Furthermore, the approach toward the study of competence taken here is constructivist (Piaget, 1970) or constitutive (Garfinkel, 1963; Mehan and Wood, 1975) because it is aimed at delineating some of the practices involved in the production of the normative order. As such, it contrasts with the more interpersonal view adopted by Weinsten (1969) and O'Malley (1977), who are concerned with "productive and mutually satisfying interactions between a child and peers or adults" (O'Malley, 1977:29; compare Clement, 1977).

COMPETENCE AS MEMBERSHIP IN A SOCIETY   This definition of interactional competence as participation or membership in a classroom follows previous discussions of membership in a society. Some of the origins of this position are to be found in Tylor's (1871:1) description of culture: "Culture or civilization, taken in its widest ethnographic sense, is that complex whole which includes knowledge, belief, art, morals, law, custom, or any other capabilities and habits acquired by man as a member of society." This definition of culture was meant to distinguish those aspects of the totality of human existence that are social and transmitted by symbolic means from those aspects that are biological and transmitted by genetic means. This "omnibus" conception of culture has been constrained somewhat by Goodenough (1964, 1976). On one occasion, he wrote, "As I see it, a society's culture consists of whatever one has to know or believe in order to operate in a manner acceptable to its members, and to do so in any role that they may accept for themselves" (1964:36). More recently, he said, "[The] culture of any society is made up of the concepts, beliefs, and principles of action and organization that an ethnographer had found he could attribute successfully to the members of society in the context of his dealings with them" (1976:3). "His competence is indicated by his ability to interact effectively in its terms with others who are already competent" (1976:4).

These formulations are helpful because they provide a rationale or warrant for the conception of competence as the requisites for effective participation in a community. However, we must be on guard here against both an overly mentalistic and an overly behavioristic conception of competence.

The concept of culture provided by Goodenough and "ethnoscientists" (Studevent, 1964) has a strong cognitive orientation. It can lead unwittingly to the position that competence is only things in people's heads (ideas, beliefs, knowledge).

Interactional competence is not purely a cognitive or subjectivistic consideration. It is not to be confused with underlying abilities. The conception of competence being developed here is interactional in the sense that it is a competence that is available in the interaction. As Garfinkel (1963:190) has said, "There is no reason to look under the skull, since there is nothing of interest to be found there but brains. The skin of the person is to be left intact. Instead questions will be confined to the operations that can be performed upon events that are 'scenic' to the person."

Effective participation in interaction requires that people produce behavior and interpret behavior in a manner that is acceptable to others. This means that the patterns of behavior, the customs, the folkways, of the cultural group, need to be taken into account.

Nevertheless, it must be kept in mind that this call to consider patterns of behavior is not simply a recommendation to substitute a behavioral definition for a cognitive conception of culture or competence. Culture is not an either/or proposition: either cognition or behavior. It is neither purely objective (a pattern of action that simply exists in the world), nor purely subjective (a mental state in an individual's head). Neither cognition nor behavior can exist without the other; they are in a constant dialectical relationship.

Friere (1968) has said that separating the objective from the subjective aspects of human experiences when analyzing reality or acting upon it results in two simplistic positions. The denial of the subjective (in this case, cognition) results in objectivism—a conception of a world without people. The denial of the objective aspects of human experience (in this case, behavior), results in subjectivism, and in extreme cases, in solipcism, for it postulates people without a world.

Both of these extremes are ingenuous, for "world and people do not exist apart from each other; they exist in constant interaction" (Friere, 1968:36).

Treating culture in purely cognitive or purely behavioral terms is "alienating" in that it divorces culture from its modes of human production, the constructive or constitutive "work" that assembles human experiences. Patterns of behavior are constructed in social scenes; knowledge is displayed in interaction between people.

Coming to an understanding of interactional competence, therefore, necessitates treating culture as intersubjective praxis (that is, human productive and comprehension practices) instead of either a subjective state or an objective thing. On the one hand, this means describing what people do with their cultural knowledge, how they use what they know about social structure, norms, and other people in ongoing social situations, encounters, and events. On the other hand, it means describing the active modes of human production and construction, the concrete observable "work" of people that assembles orderly social entities. In both cases, it means recognizing that the world and people are in a constantly reflexive relationship.

Treating culture as human productive practices makes competence interactional in two senses of the term. One, it is the competence necessary for effective interaction. Two, it is the competence that is available in the interaction between participants.

LINGUISTIC AND COMMUNICATIVE COMPETENCE   This conception of interactional competence is also influenced by certain linguistic conceptions of competence. Therefore, I think it is worthwhile to spell out some of these relationships before turning attention to the study of interactional competence in actual classroom circumstances.

Chomsky (1965) is famous for characterizing "linguistic competence" as the skills and abilities that a speaker must have in order to produce and understand phonologically, grammatically, and semantically correct sentences. He proposed a generative model of linguistic skills in which a small finite number of rules was responsible for the production of a large finite number of well-formed sentences.

Hymes (1974) and other sociolinguists[1] (Ervin-Tripp, 1972; Gumperz, 1971; Labov, 1972; Shuy, Wolfram, and Riley, 1967), while tacitly accepting Chomsky's generative metaphor, have challenged grammatically based conceptions of competence for being too narrow. Linguistic competence as defined by Chomsky accounts for the generation of the possible sentences in a language, but it does not account for the occasions when they are to be used. An actual speaker-hearer of a language equipped with only that version of linguistic knowledge would be a social incompetent. That person might be observed uttering sentences continually and in a random order. That person would not know when to speak, when not to speak, what to say, with whom, in what way, when and where.

Communication involves the production of socially appropriate speech, which includes, but is not limited to, the production of grammatically correct sentences. Therefore, sociolinguists maintain that a theory of a language (and, therefore, of competence) must account for language use in discourse and social contexts, not only the production of well-formed sentences.

Sociolinguists broaden the conception of competence so that the "formal" aspects of language (the knowledge of phonology, syntax, and semantics) involved in the production of well-formed sentences are encompassed by the "functional" aspects of language (see especially Shuy and Griffin, 1978, on this point). The functional aspects of language concern effective language use in different social situations. They include the speaker-hearer's ability to accomplish tasks with language, ability to communicate and interpret intentions, knowledge of the functions that language can serve, knowledge of the strategies of language that can be used to accomplish each function, and knowledge of the constraints that social situations impose on the selection of a particular way of speaking from a person's repertoire. Hymes has coined the term "communicative competence" to refer to the capacity to acquire and use language appropriately in different social situations. Communicative competence is recommended as a more encompassing formulation of a speaker-hearer's knowledge of language than Chomsky's formal linguistic competence.

There have been a number of studies influenced by Hymes's conception of competence (Gumperz and Hymes, 1964; Bauman and Sherzer, 1974; Sanches and Blount, 1975). These studies have produced descriptions of people's ways of speaking in different social situations in contrasting cultural contexts, and of patterns of speaking in a particular group or institution within a society, such as greetings, narratives, commands, joking, and chants. In so doing, these researchers have demonstrated that an intimate relationship exists among language forms, the functions they serve in discourse, and the social contexts in which they appear.

For the most part, these studies have concentrated on the production of acts of speech. Descriptions of some of the skills and abilities involved in the production of utterances or speech acts have been produced, but the skills and abilities involved in interaction have not been the center of focus. As a result, the concept of competence in these sociolinguistic studies becomes, for all intents and purposes, "competence for speaking," not competence for interaction.

Interaction is not isomorphic with speaking. There is more to interaction than the production of sentences or utterances that are grammatically correct and socially appropriate on a particular occasion. Most notably, there is an interpretive as well as a productive aspect of interaction. Interaction involves the interpretation of the speech behavior and other behavior of people and the interpretation of setting features of social activities, including normative role statements.

The addition of the interpretive to the productive aspects of communication makes interaction a distinctively cooperative activity, larger, more encompassing than any of the parties involved. It places interaction, including conversation and other speech events, on a different ontological level than either utterances or speech acts. While utterances and speech acts are produced by solitary speakers, people participate in conversations and interactions. While the presence of an utterance as a thing-in-the-world requires only a single person, the presence of a conversation requires cooperative activity. Speaking implies hearing. Hearing, in turn, implies that other people are influential in the communicative process. Whether as so-called passive members of an audience, or as acknowledged active participants in a conversation, hearers influence the direction of discourse. They influence the speaker's selection of utterances, provide "back-channel" feedback (Duncan, 1972), and thereby collectively produce those interactional events called conversations, speeches, debates, and so on.

Interactional Competence in the Classroom

Now that I have provided this background to my conception of interactional competence, it is time to ask what competent membership in the classroom community involves. What must students know and do in order to be judged as effective or successful in the eyes of other members of the classroom community, especially the teacher?

Competent membership in the classroom community obviously involves academic skills and abilities. To be successful in the classroom, students must indeed master academic subject matter. They must learn to read, write, and compute. They must learn the content of such subjects as history, social studies, and science.

But classroom competence is not limited to academic matters. As I will show, classroom competence involves matters of form as well as of content. To be successful in the classroom, students not only must know the content of academic subjects, they must learn the appropriate form in which to cast their academic knowledge. That is, competent membership in the classroom community involves employing interactional skills and abilities in the display of academic knowledge. They must know with whom, when, and where they can speak and act, and they must provide the speech and behavior that are appropriate for a given classroom situation. Students must also be able to relate behavior, both academic and social, to varying classroom situations by interpreting implicit classroom rules.

There are three parts to this analysis of students' competent participation in lessons. The first has to do with the work involved in the production of academically correct and interactionally appropriate behavior. The second has to do with the students' rights for initiating new topics. The third, which cuts across the first two, deals with the work involved in interpreting teachers' instructions about preferred patterns of action.

The Production of Academically Correct and Interactionally Appropriate Responses

THE INTEGRATION OF FORM AND CONTENT   I have described classroom lessons as composed of a series of initiation-reply-evaluation sequences between teachers and students. Most of these sequences are initiated by the teacher (see table 2.1 in chapter 2). The teacher provides information to the students, elicits information from them, and directs their actions. Certain replies are called for and others are denied by these initiation acts. Effective participation in classroom lessons involves providing the kind of reply that is consistent with the teacher's initiation.

When the teacher is providing students with information in the form of a lecture or opening remarks (such as 3:3, "Ok, this is some work for people in these rows of chairs"), students must know to be attentive and not engage in any overt behavior. When the teacher directs students to take procedural action (such as 4:41, "Uh, Jerome, could you move back so everyone can see?"), they must know to take that action. When the teacher is eliciting information, the students must provide the kind of information demanded by the elicitation. They must be able to provide factual information when asked "what is this?" (3:6), "I called the tractor a mmm . . . " (5:13), or "anybody, whose name is this?" (4:46). They must be able to choose the appropriate reply from a prearranged list when asked "which one is that one?" (7:24); give opinions when asked "why do you like the middle one?" (7:26); and provide the grounds of their reasoning when asked, for example, "How, Sabrina, did you remember that?" (5:19). That is, effective participation in classroom lessons involves distinguishing between directive, informative, and elicitation speech acts and providing the proper replies (re-actions, acknowledgments, and responses) on the right occasions in order to produce symmetry between initiation and reply acts.

There are additional constraints on students when the teacher initiates action. As the teacher is eliciting informa-tion from students, she is simultaneously allocating turns to them (see chapter 3). Under normal classroom circum-stances, the teacher allocates turns by nominating individual students, by inviting students to bid for the floor, or by in-viting direct replies. Each of these procedures proscribes dif-ferent behavior. On some occasions pupils can reply directly, while on others they must receive permission to reply. To contribute successfully to classroom lessons, students must discriminate among the subtleties of these normative proce-dures. When one particular student has been awarded the floor by name or by nonverbal means, other students must know to be silent. When the teacher invites bids for the floor, students must know to raise their hands and not shout out the answers. When the teacher invites replies from the class, students must realize they can contribute directly. Those who misinterpret an invitation to reply as an invitation to bid, and raise their hands instead of answering, lose the opportunity to display what they know.

When these two dimensions of classroom discourse, form and content, are integrated, interaction between teacher and students proceeds smoothly. Students reply to teachers' re-quests for information, listen attentively to informative com-ments, and respond to procedural requests. Students raise their hands when invitations to bid are made and reply in unison when invitations to reply are made.

THE SEPARATION OF FORM AND CONTENT However, not all interaction in classroom lessons conforms to this nor-mative ideal. Students do not always synchronize what they know with these normative procedures for the display of aca-demic knowledge. The separation of form and content leads to inappropriate social displays in the classroom and negative evaluations by the teacher. This is as much the case for the student who provides correct academic content without the appropriate social form as it is for the student who provides appropriate form without correct content.

Content without form. The student who supplies correct academic information but does not use appropriate turn-taking procedures typifies the case of content without form.

Initiation	Reply	Evaluation
3:15 T: Now, what can you think, can you think of something to eat?	Many: Snakes.	T: Wait a minute, wait a minute.
	Many: (raise hands) Snakes.	T: Wait a minute, raise your hand. Raise your hand. Give people a chance to think.
4:93 T: Um, who can think of some words (draws on board)?	Many: Jelly, Jerome.	T: Martin, raise your hand to give other people a chance to think. That's why I want you to raise your hand, to give other people a chance to think.

These students knew the correct answers to the teacher's questions, but they did not employ the correct procedures for gaining access to the floor. The teacher had invited students to bid for the floor. However, the students replied directly. Consequently, their actions were negatively evaluated by the teacher.

Form without content. Once students have gained access to the floor, they must know what to do with it. The student who has mastered the procedures for gaining access to the floor but does not have simultaneous command over academic information typifies the case of form without content.

Initiation	Reply	Evaluation
4:46	Jeannie: (raises hand)	
4:47 T: Jeannie.	Jeannie: (pauses) I had it and I lost it.	T: Uh, ya.

It appears in this case that the student knew that hand raising was an important aspect of classroom participation, but that she had not yet learned that supplying information is an integral accompaniment to that activity. This student knew how to gain access to the floor, but did not know what to do with it once she had it.

A similar lack of congruence between the form and content of students' replies occurs when students bid for the floor before a teacher has completed asking a question. The following example is from the opening of the Cafeteria Trays lessons.

Initiation	Reply	Evaluation
7:1 T: Um, now, uh, let me ask you about something about lunch. You people have been doing a		

Initiation	Reply	Evaluation
very good job as I said yesterday, about walking to the cafeteria and back without cutting.		
	Jeannie: (raises hand)	
	Many: Uh huh.	
7:2 T: That part's been ok, right, Prenda.	Prenda: Yeah.	
7:3 T: We're still not so good about coming back into the room. Um, but the, but the cutting isn't, the no-cutting is really worked well.	Jeannie: (raises hand) Jeannie: (raises hand)	
7:4 T: Now let me ask you something about in the cafeteria. Somebody has to take your trays and empty them, and put them //	//Jeannie: (raises hand) Jeannie: (lowers hand)	T: Wait a minute, let me finish, let me ask the question.

Each time the teacher paused for breath, a student raised her hand. Finally, exasperated, the teacher rebuked that student for not synchronizing her bid for the floor with the completion of her initiation.

There are practical consequences for students who do not unite form and content. If a student provides correct content without proper form, that student will be reprimanded. A history of such inappropriate behavior can lead the teacher to treat the student negatively. If a student attends to form without an equivalent concern for content, that student loses opportunities to express knowledge. A history of lost opportunities can lead a teacher to believe that a student is inattentive, unexpressive, and the like. It is in this arena that teachers' expectations can be built up, and worked out interactionally.

In sum, effective participation in classroom lessons involves the integration of interactional skills and academic knowledge. Students have a repertoire of academic information and social knowledge available to them. To display this knowledge when the teacher initiates action, they must be able to choose a reply from their repertoire that is appropriate for the occasion. When the teacher is allocating the floor to students, they must recognize the turn-allocation procedure that is operating and provide the behavior that is consistent with those normative expectations. Once students have gained access to the floor, they must synchronize the appropriate form of their reply with the correct content.

Students' Initiation Rights

Although teacher-initiated action predominates in classroom lessons, the students' role is not limited to replying when called upon. Contrary to more mechanistic conceptions of classroom interaction, which assume that the direction of action flows exclusively from the teacher to the student (see Dunkin and Biddle, 1974; chap. 12, for a sampling), close observation of teacher-student interaction reveals evidence of mutual influence in classroom relationships: students influencing teachers while teachers influence students. Notable in this regard are the "mediating strategies" (Doyle, 1978) that students use to initiate action during lessons.

THE INTERACTIONAL WORK OF STUDENT CONTRIBUTIONS   There seem to be three component parts involved in having student contributions incorporated into the course of a lesson: (1) getting the floor, (2) holding the floor, and (3) introducing news. Dynamic interactional work is represented by each of these components.

Getting the floor. Having a turn to talk is the minimal requisite for influencing the course of a lesson. This involves getting the floor. However, students cannot just talk any time. There are proper places for students to introduce their talk. Therefore, locating an appropriate floor-control juncture is a component skill in students' contributions to classroom lessons.

Although in ordinary, everyday conversation, speaker-change points can potentially occur after every speaker's turn (Sacks, Schegloff, and Jefferson, 1974), this state of affairs does not exist in classroom conversation. When the teacher initiates action, she allocates the floor, the students reply, and the teacher takes the floor back again as she evaluates the reply. That set of actions constitutes an integral unit, which means that the appropriate juncture for students to gain access to the floor is after an initiation-reply-evaluation sequence, not after any speaker turn.

The basic initiation-reply-evaluation format of classroom lessons can be conceptualized for our purposes as a series of turns of talk separated by junctures. A turn of talk is a string of utterances spoken by one person between other persons' talk (see Sacks, Schegloff, and Jefferson, 1974). A juncture is a break (silence) between turns of talk (see Birdwhistell, 1970; Kendon, 1970; Scheflen, 1972). Although for practical reasons, our transcript style (Mehan et al., 1976) displays these sequences of sounds and silences one under the other, the actual flow of talk is more chronological, as illustrated in figure 4.1.
When our earlier analytic is superimposed on this schema, turn I is an initiation act, turn II is a reply act, turn III is an evaluation act, and so on.

When the teacher initiates action, the students reply, and the teacher evaluates. In such cases, the next possible junc-

FIGURE 4.1. CLASSROOM LESSONS DEPICTED AS
CHRONOLOGICAL TURNS OF TALK.

Turn I		Turn II		Turn III		Turn IV
sound (turn of talk)	silence (juncture)	*sound* (turn of talk)	silence (juncture)	*sound* (turn of talk)	silence (juncture)	*sound* (turn of talk)

ture for a student to gain control of the floor for the purposes of contributing his or her topics is between turn III and turn IV. Figure 4.2, which modifies figure 4.1 by identifying speech acts and associated speakers, displays this possible floor-control juncture.

During the course of the year, the students became sophisticated in locating these "seams" in the essentially teacher-controlled discourse. Their mastery of this aspect of the turn-allocation machinery eventually enabled them to contribute their own information to the lessons.

At first, students did not distinguish junctures between completed initiation-reply-evaluation sequences (between turns III and IV) from junctures within sequences (between turns I and II or II and III). They indiscriminately attempted to add information in the middle of ongoing sequences. The following example is from the first week of school.

FIGURE 4.2. CLASSROOM LESSONS WITH SPEECH ACTS AND TURNS COMBINED.

	Turn I		Turn II		Turn III		Turn IV
	sound	silence	*sound*	silence	*sound*	silence	*sound*
Speaker	teacher		student		teacher or student		teacher or student
Act	initiation		reply		evaluation		initiation

Initiation	Reply	Evaluation
4:50 T: Now, Jerome, tell us what you put on the map yesterday.	Jerome: The office, the office.	T: Jerome, put the steps and the door//Carolyn: and the door//T: right up to the office.
4:51 Carolyn: It ain't open.		Jerome: It is open. T: He made it, he wanted to show it open//Carolyn: I know//T: and it's just in the right place.

As the teacher formulated Jerome's contribution to the map of the schoolyard, Carolyn added commentary in the middle of the teacher's talk (4:50), and attempted to challenge facts about the drawing. Both the teacher and Jerome rebuffed her intrusion.

Another example of a student attempting to introduce information in the middle of an ongoing sequence occurred in the Map Words lesson, also conducted during the first week of school. The teacher placed word cards on the floor before the students and invited them to identify ones they knew.

Initiation	Reply	Evaluation
5:66 T: Uh, all right, we've got three words left. Who		

Initiation	Reply	Evaluation
could put one of those . . . (points to cards)	Everett: (raises hand)	
5:67 T: Um, which one, go ahead, which one can . . .	Everett: (moves toward board)	T: All right.
5:68 T: Where's that word?	Everett: (places word card on board)	Edward: He can't find it.
		T: He'll find it, he'll find it.

Edward commented on Everett's attempt to place a card on the storyboard. The teacher rebuffed his intrusion.

These attempts to gain the floor were not successful because the students attempted to insert new information into the middle of an ongoing sequence of interaction. The reactions of the other participants mark these as intrusions into the established order. Thus, one appropriate place to introduce new information is at the completion of an initiation-reply-evaluation sequence, not in the middle of an ongoing sequence.

The following sequences show that the completion of an initiation-reply-evaluation sequence is not automatically an appropriate turn-control juncture. As I showed in the discussion of extended sequences (chapter 2), if a topic introduced in turn I (see figures 4.1 and 4.2) by the teacher has not been completed by turn III, the floor still belongs to the teacher. She continues to allocate the floor until the initial topic is completed. The presence of extended sequences of interac-

tion in classroom lessons suggests that another appropriate
turn-control juncture occurs at the end of topically related
sets.

The following sequence from the *S* and *M* Words lesson
illustrates this point. The teacher had just asked students to
suggest words that started with the letter *S*.

Initiation	Reply	Evaluation
3:33 T: Ok, um, what else can you think of that starts with this letter (points to *S* on board), salad, and sandwich . . .	Jerome: And Ssss.	T: Wait a minute.
3:34 Jerome: Could we make a snake on there?		T: Wait a minute.
3:35 Jerome: Not to eat.		T: Not to eat, yes, you can make a snake but not to eat.

After Jerome provided an incorrect reply (3:33), he attempted
to introduce a new topic.·The teacher sanctioned his attempt
to change the course of the lesson before accepting snake as
an "S word."[2]

After the teacher had completed the phase of the Martin
Luther King lesson that dealt with people's ages, she an-
nounced that she was going to begin reading the story:

Initiation	Reply	Evaluation
9:71 T: I'm just going to start this story on		

Initiation	Reply	Evaluation
Martin Luther King//		
9:72 //Greg: Well, my mama was 19 when he died.		T: (touches Greg's knee)

In these examples, the students had begun to initiate action after an initiation-reply-evaluation sequence. Since the topic established in these sequences was not completed, the teacher sanctioned the students' initiations as an interruption of the previously established topic. These examples suggest that getting the floor consists of recognizing the completion of interactional sequences and the completion of instructional topics.

As the following examples demonstrate, students increasingly made that distinction as the year progressed.

Initiation	Reply	Evaluation
9:71 T: I'm just going to start this story on Martin Luther King//		
9:72 //Greg: Well, my mama was 19 when he died.		T: (touches Greg's knee)
9:73 T: and then we'll go on with this later in the day.		

Greg attempted to introduce information about his mother's age (9:72). The teacher touched his knee as a way of sanctioning his attempt to introduce this topic, and continued with her announcement.

At one point during the namecards lesson, the teacher asked Jerome to identify a namecard (4:31). After he responded incorrectly, the teacher asked other students to reply:

Initiation	Reply	Evaluation
4:33 T: (still holding up same card)	Everett: Everett.	
	Carolyn: Edward.	T: Edward, good for you, Carolyn.

4:34
Jerome: That's what I
    was going to say.
		T: Everett, it begins
		    like your name,
		    doesn't it? That's
		    why at first you
		    thought it was
		    yours and then you
		    knew, corrected it.
		    (lowers card)

Everett and Carolyn replied, Everett incorrectly, Carolyn correctly. The teacher complimented Carolyn for her work. At this point (4:34) Jerome provided information about his work. Jerome placed his informative in the proper place in the sequence (after an initiation-reply-evaluation sequence was completed). Unlike the attempts to gain access to the floor discussed above, this informative was not negatively evaluated. It was allowed to pass.

Later that morning, after the teacher had finished marking the place on the map where Leola was to draw her house, Jerome introduced a comment:

Initiation	Reply	Evaluation
4:77 T: But I think we ought to wait and let Leola, until Leola (prints Leola's name) comes and //Carolyn: (spells) L-E-O-L-A//T: Let her put her house, right?	Many: (nod yes)	
4:78 J: I should put in my house.		
4:79 T: Um, what color should we make the street? (touches street on map)		

This comment was also placed on the floor without negative evaluation by the teacher. The teacher worked around it, initiating a new sequence of elicitations dealing with the color of the street on the map (see Mehan et al., 1976, 4:79-82).

A variation of this sequence often occurred when the teacher was momentarily "away" (Goffman, 1961) from the class. While presenting materials to the students during lessons, the teacher sometimes turned her back on the class to write on the board (S and J Words lesson, Whistle for Willy) or to pin information to a map (Map Words and Birthplaces lessons). She also averted her attention when she focused on materials held in her lap (Namecards and Birthplaces lessons). The students became skillful at getting into the lesson during those times when the teacher was "away."

The following sequence is representative. During the Birth-places lesson, the teacher engaged Martha in a discussion about her family (8:53-77). After she marked Martha's birth-place on the map, she attempted to learn about other members of Martha's family:

Initiation	Reply	Evaluation
8:55 T: It says Martha's father was born in Mexico.		
8:56 C: Right here. (pointing to the map) T: (write on paper)		
8:57 E: So it's by Mexico.		
8:58 Michael: I betcha mine's going to be Mexico.		
8:59 Miguel: Mine too.		
8:60 T: Martha's father now, this isn't a very good map of Mexico, Martha, cuz it doesn't have cities, so I don't know if I'm putting it in the right place, but I'm just going to put it down here in Mexico.		
8:61 C: You have to have		

Initiation	Reply	Evaluation
other cities.		
8:62 T: And your mother was born in Kansas.		

As the teacher wrote new information on the paper in her lap, the students provided commentary (8:57-59). The teacher momentarily returned her attention to the class to report about Martha's father's birthplace (8:60). When she turned to place a pin on the map, Carolyn inserted still more information.

These snippets of interaction suggest that getting the floor consists of recognizing the completion of interactional sequences, including the completion of instructional topics. As the year progressed, students increasingly distinguished the proper slots to insert talk and other behavior. They progressed from indiscriminately inserting talk into the middle of ongoing sequences to introducing ideas at the end of topically coherent sequences. Teachers' sanctions of students' misplaced intrusions declined slightly across the year, from 10 percent of all student-initiated sequences during the first week of school to 8 percent in the fall and 6 percent in the winter. The dominant form of student-initiated sequences in the early fall was a student informative followed by silence from other classroom participants. That is, when students gained access to the floor without sanction, they were able to introduce topics, but the topics they presented were not picked up by others. Instead, these student initiations were ignored by the teacher and other students. This pattern was evident in 70 percent of student initiations in the S and J Words lessons, and in 53 percent of student initiations in the Namecards, Map, S and M Words, and Whistle for Willy lessons, all conducted in early fall. The frequency of this pattern decreased during the year. Only 41 percent of student initiations were ignored in the Birthplaces lesson conducted in November, and this figure decreased to 28.5 percent in the Martin Luther King lesson conducted in January.

Holding the floor. A researcher only computing the frequency of occurrences of teacher and student talk (such as Flanders, 1970) might conclude that these data indicate that students talk often during these lessons. However, a simple quantification analysis would overlook the fact that these students' talk, although appearing in a proper place, received no responses from others.

Locating appropriate floor-control junctures is a necessary component of effective participation in classroom lessons. However, simply getting talk on the floor is not sufficient. Students must not only get their talk on the floor, they must have their contributions picked up by others as well (Philips, 1974).

The students' mastery of the subtleties involved in holding the floor is illustrated in the following examples. Near the end of the *S* and *M* Words lesson, the teacher asked the students to recapitulate the words they had offered previously that started with the letters *S* and *M*. After an initial list was produced, the teacher encouraged the students to give still more words:

Initiation	Reply	Evaluation
3:52 T: And what else?	Many: Potato salad, potato salad.	T: Salad, sandwich.
	___: Potato salad.	
	Audrey: Snake.	T: Snake, good, good, Audrey, you remembered.
3:53 C: But you can't eat it.		T: No, you can't eat it, but anything that begins with an *S*— that's right you can't eat it.

After the teacher complimented Audrey for her contribution, Carolyn interjected a comment on Audrey's reply. Carolyn placed her informative at a proper juncture in the lesson. It did not disrupt the symmetry of the sequence that was in progress. Unlike the information described in the previous section, which was properly placed yet ignored by other classroom participants, Carolyn's comment was picked up by the teacher. She specifically responded to Carolyn's initiation act. Her treatment of this informative was brief, however; she provided only the minimal requisite response. She did not pursue this student's topic; rather she continued to request more words for her summary (see Mehan et al., 1976, 3:54).

In effect, the teacher has "bound off" Carolyn's contribution. This treatment of some students' initiations properly placed on the floor is also visible in the following sequence. While the teacher was reading the story about Martin Luther King's childhood to the class, a student interrupted to ask a question:

Initiation	Reply	Evaluation
9:77 __: _____		T: What?
9:78 V: Ten speed bicycle.		T: I don't think it was a ten speed bicycle in those days, Victor, ten speed bicycles are newer, and uh, they didn't have a lot of money, the King family.

Like her treatment of Carolyn's comment on the inedibility of snakes, the teacher's response to Victor's interest in the models of bicycles in King's day was fleeting.

These students displayed some, but not all, of the necessary skills for successful influence over the course of lessons. They were able to gain access to the floor successfully. They were able to contribute some information of their own choosing. But their time on the floor was momentary and fleeting. Their topics did not alter the course of the teacher's lesson agenda.

An examination of the quality of these and similar initiation acts reveals the reason for this. The initiation acts that were picked up but then bounded off by the teacher all commented on the previous topics in lessons. They did not add anything new to the discussion.

Introducing news. In order for a student's contribution to change the course of a lesson once it is in progress, it must not only be placed in the proper juncture, and be relevant to previous discussion, it must make an "interesting" (compare Davis, 1971) or "original" contribution as well. The addition of this component to the others enabled students to gain control of the lesson format. There was ample evidence of this combination of skills (competence) throughout both the Birthplaces and the Martin Luther King lessons, which were conducted near the middle of the year.

After the teacher determined that Martha's mother was born in Kansas (8:62), she initiated a sequence of interactions in which she encouraged the students to locate that state on the map. Roberto completed this task successfully (8:65). As the teacher was writing this information on a card in her lap, a number of students introduced information that reached the floor but was not picked up by the teacher. Then Carolyn made the following observation:

Initiation	Reply	Evaluation
8:71 C: Teacher, it's across from Arkansas.		
8:72 __: _____Kansas.		T: Um, um, wait a

Initiation	Reply	Evaluation
		minute.
8:73 T: Carolyn, what do you mean?		
8:74 T: Are you ready to come and join us in the circle?		
8:75 E: It's close to Arkansas.		
8:76 T: Um, Carolyn, what did you mean by it's across from Arkansas?	C: Cuz you can see Arkansas right next to it.	T: Yeah.

The teacher treated this student's informative differently than any of the others we have considered so far. She neither ignored nor "bounded it off." Instead, she worked very hard to encourage Carolyn's observation. She "closed out" another student's attempt to gain the floor (8:72), directed a disruptive student's attention (8:74), and ignored Edward's observation (8:75) in order to give Carolyn further opportunities to express herself (8:76). Carolyn's observation was incorporated into the lesson because her observation was unique. It introduced genuinely new information.

This characteristic also accounts for the students' success in introducing the topic of the teacher's birthplace later in this lesson.

In the middle of a series of questions about students' birthplaces, the teacher asked Roberto where he was born; after he declined to answer (8:109), Wallace spoke:

Initiation	Reply	Evaluation
8:110 W: Teacher, where were you born?	T: Wh, I'm going to tell you.	

Based on our interpretation of the hesitancy in her voice as she replied, the teacher seemed to be surprised by this question. She responded by putting Wallace "on hold," while she continued through the topics on her agenda about Roberto's family (8:111-116), and dealt with a request to ask about Victor's family (8:117-119). Then she returned to this new topic:

Initiation	Reply	Evaluation
8:120 T: Somebody, somebody asked where I came from, and, uh, I wonder if anybody remembers?	Many: _____ Carolyn: You came from right there. Alberto: She came from Boston, Boston, Boston.	T: Boston, Alberto, good for you, you remembered I said Boston.

Immediately after this exchange, other students demonstrated their competence at introducing new topics. Edward asked about Boston's location (8:121); his question led to a search on the map (8:112-125) and an examination of how students knew its location (8:126). Carolyn followed her introduction of the topic of one teacher's birthplace with a similar question about the other teacher's birthplace:

Initiation	Reply	Evaluation
8:128 C: Teacher, teacher, ask Ms. Coles, tell us where you were born. Ms. Coles, where were you born?	Many: (talking out) T: All right, there's a card in here for Ms. Coles too.	
8:129 W: Ms. Coles, where was you born Ms. Coles? Where was you born?		
8:130 T: Where did, where did you come from?	Ms. C: I was born in Virginia.	T: Virginia, okay, Virginia.

Similar questions were asked about the student aide's birthplace and its location on the map:

Initiation	Reply	Evaluation
8:134 W: Where was you born jungle Jim, Jim, George?		
8:135 T: Okay, Mr. Munoz, since you're here today, where did you come from?	Mr. M: I came from	

Initiation	Reply	Evaluation
	Chula Vista.	Ms. C: Hey, Chula Vista, Chula Vista.
		Carolyn: Chula Vista, we can't . . .
		T: That's too fine a differentiation for this map. (writes on card)
8:136 W: Where's Chula Vista?	C: I don't know, but wherever it is, come on.	
	T: Uh, if this were a map of California, and we'll get one some day, Chula Vista would be in between San Diego and Tijuana.	
	M: (pointing) Right here.	
	T: It would be here, in between, ah, San Diego and the border (pins card on map).	

These students were very successful in introducing their own topics into the lesson, and changing its course in the process. Their success seems to be attributable to their ability to introduce interesting topics at the right junctures in the lesson.

Wallace displayed the same skill in the Martin Luther King

lesson. Just at the point when the teacher completed determining the students' ages at the time of King's death, Wallace asked about the teacher's age. That question, although an interruption of the teacher's agenda, was incorporated into the lesson by the teacher. That question also produced an extended sequence that traversed a number of turns of talk between teacher and students:

Initation	Reply	Evaluation
9:62 T: Now//		

9:63
  //W: How old are
      you?
	T: Ah hah!//
	
	//G: She was 23
	      years old.//	

9:64
  T: I, I'll, uh, I'll tell
    you my age, ah,
    Wallace and you
    see, and you
    figure.		

9:65 C: 22?	T: No, I'm 49.	
9:66 G: Huh?		
9:67 T: Now how//		

9:68
  C: Huh?
	T: I know, that
	    seems very
	    ancient.
	
	__: 50.	

Initiation	Reply	Evaluation
	M: 40.	T: 49.
9:69 T: Now 7 years ago, how old was I?	G: Are you 48?	
	__: 40.	
	E: She 23.	
9:70 T: Now I'll leave you to think about that Wallace.	C: She's 23.	
9:71 T: I'm just going to start this story on Martin Luther King.		

Wallace interrupted the teacher to ask about her age (9:62-63). The teacher accepted the unexpected, and asked Wallace to compute that figure (9:64). After ignoring a number of guesses by other students (9:65-68), the teacher began reading the story. After a considerable time, Wallace bid for the teacher's attention:

Initiation	Reply	Evaluation
9:79 T: (nods to Wallace)	W: You were 41. (lowers hand)	T: Uh, 49 take away 7, pretty close.
	G: 42.	T: Yeah, 42 is right, Greg.

Receiving the floor (9:79), Wallace produced his reply. His computation was wrong, and Greg supplied the teacher's correct age (9:79). (See the discussion of opening the floor in chapter 3.)

This sequence also demonstrates that co-occurrence relationships extend across a considerable range of talk (see chapter 2). The topic introduced in 9:64 and enforced in 9:69 and 9:70 was finally completed nine lines later. The completion of that extended sequence, interlaced with interstitial material, conforms to the same basic format of adjacently related sequences. That is, the correct reply was accorded a favorable evaluation by the teacher (9:79).

These students too were successful in introducing their own topics and changing the course of the lesson, apparently because of their ability to introduce interesting topics at the right junctures in the lesson.

THE PATTERNS OF STUDENTS' CONTRIBUTIONS   Having contributions incorporated into lessons involves inserting information in the appropriate junctures, choosing topics relevant to the previous course of discussion, and making original contributions. If students do not integrate all of these components, they neither sustain control over the floor nor change the course of the lesson. If students attempt to initiate action without taking junctures into account, they will be sanctioned. If they introduce information at the appropriate juncture but do not tie this information to previous topics, their comments will be ignored completely. If they introduce information at the appropriate juncture and tie this information to previous topics, these comments will be picked up by others, but bounded off. When students weave all of these skills together, they successfully introduce their topics into lessons.

There is ample evidence that the students in this classroom learned the structure of these lessons as the year progressed. First of all, the total number of students' contributions increased during the year. Students initiated 10.0 percent of the sequences in lessons conducted in September, 4.6 percent in October, 4.1 percent in November, and 31.4 percent in January. Second, the quality of student-initiated interactional sequences changed across the year. This increase in sophistication can be seen in the decline of the teacher's sanction of inappropriate students' actions, the decline of student-initiated acts that were ignored by others, and the significant increase in student initiations that were incorporated into lessons.

These changes in the social organization of student-initiated exchanges are summarized in table 4.1. These figures point to a steady gain in the students' mastery of the interactional machinery driving classroom lessons. They also reinforce the view that effective classroom participation involves the integration of academic content and interactional form.

The Interpretation of Normative Demands in the Classroom

I have described the component skills involved in the production of successful responses and students' initiation rights in the classroom lessons. In addition to these communicative skills, interpretive skills are required for competent participation in the classroom community.

TACIT RULES   Although the teacher's practical concern is classroom order (see chapter 3), the rules that are part of this normative order are not communicated directly to the stu-

TABLE 4.1. STUDENTS' CONTRIBUTIONS TO CLASSROOM LESSONS.

Lesson	Percentage of students' initiations				
	Sanctioned	Ignored	Bound off	Incorporated	Other
S and M Words	10.0	70.0	10.0	—	10.0
Namecards	20.0	20.0	60.0	—	—
Map	—	63.6	27.2	9.2	—
S and J Words	—	100.0	—	—	—
Map Words	—	—	100.0	—	—
Cafeteria Trays	—	—	100.0	—	—
Birthplaces	8.0	41.0	12.0	39.0	—
Martin Luther King	5.9	28.5	17.0	48.5	—

dents. Classroom procedures, like other normative rules, are tacit (Garfinkel, 1967; Cicourel, 1973; Cicourel et al., 1974; Mehan and Wood, 1975). They are seldom formulated by the teacher at the beginning of the school year or school day. They are not posted on the bulletin board or stated in so many words at the beginning of a classroom lesson.

More specifically, students do not hear the co-occurrence rule that the initiation and reply acts go together stated directly. The teacher does not say, "Each of my initiations calls for certain replies and not others. When I ask a question, I expect a certain kind of reply. When I lecture you, or introduce a lesson, you are not to initiate action. When I give you a list of answers, I want you to choose one, not comment on the question or offer an opinion of your own. But when I ask you 'what do you think?' then you can provide your own opinion. When I ask you 'how did you know that?' you are to tell me the reasoning that you employed to arrive at your answer."

Likewise, students are provided with information about the appropriate ways to gain access to the floor implicitly. The teacher does not say, "When I name a student by name, or nod at him or her, that student and only that student can reply. When I say 'raise your hand' or 'who knows,' students are to indicate that they know the answer by raising their hands. When I say 'what is this?' or trail off a sentence, or say 'anyone,' then everyone can answer directly."

Instead, students hear statements that *index* the existence of classroom rules. Teachers' statements like "raise your hand," "who knows," "wait a minute," or "give others a chance to think" are not the classroom rules per se; they are statements that index the rules. The rule is orderliness. The students have to abstract from the information given in implicit statements to the classroom rule.

Such statements appear retrospectively and prospectively (Schutz, 1962; Garfinkel, 1967; Cicourel, 1973) in relation to classroom action. They appear retrospectively when a student performs an act that the teacher defines as a violation of classroom procedure:

Initiation	Reply	Evaluation
4:36 T: Uh, whose name// (raises namecard)	//Jerome: Sabrina.//	
	C: Sabrina.	T: Raise your hand, raise your hand to give other people a chance to read it.
4:93 T: (begins to draw J and S on board). Um, who can think of some words . . . (continues to draw)	Many: Jelly, Jerome.	
	Carolyn: (raises, hand)	T: Martin, raise your hand to give other people a chance to think. That's why I want you to raise your hand, to give other people a chance to think.

On these occasions, "raise your hand" serves as a retrospective evaluation of the immediate past action of the students. The statement "raise your hand" or "wait a minute" indicates that a certain classroom procedure should have been in effect but was not. The retrospective appearance of a procedural statement requires the students to engage in interpretive work. They must assign meaning backward through time in order to know what the preferred state of affairs should have been then, and should be under similar circumstances in the future.

Statements like "raise your hand" are also used prospectively to indicate that a certain classroom procedure will now be in effect:

Initiation	Reply	Evaluation
4:70 T: Raise your hand if you know where Leola's house would go on this map.	Many: (raise hands)	
3:8 T: Ok, now, raise your hand. What can you think of first of all whose name in this room begins with this letter. Raise your hand, any children whose name begins with this letter. (points to S)	Jerome: (raises hand)	

The prospective appearance of procedural statements also requires the students to engage in interpretive work. Since the temporal parameters of such procedures are not stated, the duration of their effect must be decided from occasion to occasion.

Because classroom procedures are not stated in so many words, students must infer the appropriate ways to engage in classroom discourse from contextually provided information. Even if the rules of the classroom could be posted, the list would have an open horizon of meaning (Schutz, 1962; Garfinkel, 1967; Cicourel, 1973), as the rules would have to be interpreted by teachers and students in constantly changing classroom situations.

Rule-guided behavior. These findings provide further reasons to reconsider the stock sociological conception of rule-guided behavior. Various versions of stimulus-response theory and Parsons's (1937) "voluntaristic model of action" are often brought to mind at the mention of rules guiding behavior. Such theories adopt a "maximal constraint" position on the relationship between rules and behavior. They hold that human behavior is strictly determined by rules and that the rules are located in the environment. Such theories seem to leave little room for individual creativity or initiative, or for social change.

When interaction is examined closely in interactional settings, behavior does not appear to be guided by rules in this deterministic sense. In the study of human language, for example, the kinds of rules required to describe the production of sentences are beyond the capabilities of stimulus-response theories (Chomsky, 1957). As has been shown here, a parallel may be drawn to human action. Unlike a dog responding to an experimenter's light or bell, people do not respond to social rules automatically. The normative rules of society can be broken and are broken by people on a regular basis. The fact of exceptions and deviations from normative rules speaks to the creative aspects of human action. Furthermore, the normative rules of society require interpretation. While the complexity of human action cannot be captured by deterministic formulations of rules, this does not say that human behavior is beyond any description in terms of rules. Human behavior is not random or haphazard; it has structure, it is influenced by collective interests and the consideration of others.

Indeed, human behavior can be described in terms of constitutive or generative rules. To return to the case of human language, the number of possible sentences in each human language is infinite, or at least is a large finite number. Language users cannot possibly learn or store in memory the necessary formal (syntactic, semantic, phonological) or functional (strategies, functions, forms) information in list-like form. It seems as though linguistic productions are generated by a small set of functional and formal organizational principles. These principles may be considered constitutive rules (Garfinkel, 1963; Searle, 1969).

Constitutive rules compose an activity; they make the organization of an enterprise possible. Without constitutive rules, the activity can not exist. The rules of chess or some other human activity are constitutive in that they not only account for the correct, proper, incorrect, or improper in particular moves of play but also provide for the possibility of chess being chess and not "practice," or some other game like checkers or Go.

As a result, it is perhaps more heuristic to talk about people *using* rules instead of *following* them. This view (compare Wittgenstein, 1952) recognizes that rules do not serve as "springs for action" (Mills, 1940), where people blindly and mechanically follow normative prescriptions. Instead, people participate in the construction of courses of action by referring to and invoking rules, often after the fact.

Ambiguous instructions. In addition to being tacit, teachers' instructions are ambiguous. They often contain mixed signals about which actions students are expected to take.

This feature of classroom instructions can be exemplified by reference to the classroom turn-allocation procedures. The facticity of a classroom conversation is dependent upon its production by teachers and students. Turn-allocation procedures govern the appearance of a next speaker at transition points in the lesson. The continuity of the lesson depends on the participants' recognition of the particular turn-allocation procedure in operation at any given time, the participants' recognition of the appropriate transition point, and the production of appropriate behavior (talk or gesture) at that juncture.

However, teachers' instructions often contain mixed signals about which turn-allocation procedure is in operation at any given time. As a result, students must infer which of many possible procedures to follow from paralinguistic, kinesic, and contextual cues.

More specifically, on many occasions of interaction students must decide if the invitation to bid or the invitation to reply turn-allocation procedure is in effect. The invitation to bid procedure is often indexed by the teacher's utterance "who knows?" The invitation to reply procedure is often indexed by the expression "what is this?"

On some occasions, the teacher's initiation acts include both the utterance "who knows" and the utterance "what is this?" At such times, the students must determine which is the proper way to respond—replying directly or bidding for the floor. To decide, the students must attend to the paralinguistic features of the teacher's elicitation act. When she wants students to bid for the floor, she stresses the "who knows" portion of her utterance. When a direct reply is acceptable, she stresses the "what is this" portion of her utterance.

On other occasions, the students must determine if the individual nomination or invitation to reply turn-allocation procedure is in effect. To do so, they must interpret the nonverbal behavior of the teacher and the intended referent of the pronoun "you." There are times when the teacher's use of "you" indicates "all of you," and other occasions when it indicates a specific person. To be competent in the classroom, students must differentiate between these different uses of the same pronoun.

The invitation to reply turn-taking procedure is realized by a *wh* question, a chorus, or a sentence completion form (see chapter 3). When any of these forms is used, the students can reply directly. The chorus form often includes the pronoun "you." At these times, the "you" indicates that all students can reply:

Initiation	Reply	Evaluation
3:18		
T: Something you like to eat.	Many: Milk, snails.	
	Jeannie: (raises hand)	
5:6		
T: Can you read that?	Many: Yes, no.	

Initiation	Reply	Evaluation
8:50 T: You just go through that border, don't you?	Many: Yeah.	
9:10 T: Now, did any of you see last night anything on television about him?	Wallace: Not me. Miguel: I did saw it.	

On other occasions, however, the teacher nominates a particular child by name on one exchange, receives a reply, and then engages that student in an extended discussion:

Initiation	Reply	Evaluation
4:10 T: Who could tell us whose namecard this is?	Carolyn: (raises hand)	
4:11 T: Carolyn.	Carolyn: Patricia.	
4:12 T: Can you point to Patricia?	Carolyn: (points to Patricia)	T: That's right.

After Carolyn answered the teacher's initial question (4:11), the teacher followed up by asking her to point to the child she had identified. Here, the students must recognize that the "you" in the teacher's elicitation (4:12) is meant for Carolyn in particular and not the class in general.

In another example, Jerome was asked about a place on the map of the schoolyard:

Initiation	Reply	Evaluation
4:74 T: Jerome, what do you think?	Jerome: That side. (pointing to the map)	
4:75 T: Come, put your hand where it should be.	Jerome: (points to map)	

Likewise, Jerome and the other students must realize that the "you" in the teacher's elicitation (4:75) is intended for Jerome and not for everyone.

On these and other occasions,[3] the teacher is holding the floor for these students by nodding her head at them, by pointing to them, by moving closer to them, and by maintaining eye contact with them. When the teacher holds the floor for a student, the others must recognize that it is not their turn or suffer the negative consequences.

There are practical consequences for students who misinterpret these subtle cues. If a student replies when a bid is expected, that student will be sanctioned. A history of such inappropriate behavior can lead the teacher to treat the student negatively. If a student bids when a reply is possible, that student loses an opportunity to express knowledge. A history of lost opportunities can lead the teacher to believe a student is inattentive, unexpressive, and the like.

Learning Classroom Lessons

The academic aspects of classroom instruction and the skills that students presumably employ to meet these academic demands are topics that have received considerable attention (see, for example, Dunkin and Biddle, 1974). Because socialization as well as education takes place in classrooms, there are interactional as well as academic aspects of classroom instruction.

The interplay of interactional demands requires students

to integrate academic knowledge with interactional skills in order to participate effectively in the classroom community. This interactional competence in the classroom operates along a communicative and an interpretive dimension.

THE COMMUNICATIVE ASPECT OF CLASSROOM PARTICIPATION In general terms, the communicative aspect of competence (Hymes, 1974) in the classroom involves knowing that certain ways of talking and acting are appropriate on some occasions and not others: knowing with whom, when, and where to speak. Although it is incumbent upon students to display what they know during lessons, they must also know *how* to display what they know. They must bring their action into synchrony with people who are already talking. To do so, classroom rules for taking turns, producing ordered utterances, making coherent topical ties, and participating in ritualized openings and closings must be negotiated.

More specifically, competent participation in classroom lessons involves the production of academically correct and interactionally appropriate replies to teacher-initiated actions and the generation of effective initiation acts. The production of factually correct and interactionally appropriate replies, in turn, involves a number of skills. Students must recognize the turn-allocation procedure that is operating in a given teacher-student exchange and provide the behavior that is consistent with those normative expectations. Students must recognize the speech act being initiated by the teacher and provide the kind of reply that maintains symmetry between initiation and reply acts.

The production of effective initiation acts also involves a number of skills. Students must first find an appropriate place to introduce their interests, and having gained access to the floor, they must maintain control over it. The former involves recognizing the completion of a prior interactional sequence and the completion of previous instructional topics. The latter involves having topics picked up by others. In order to have topics incorporated into the lesson, students need to introduce new and interesting ideas, not merely comment on the prior course of events.

This aspect of communicative competence implies that

students are active participants in the contexts in which they are acting. They are constructing their environments, not passively responding to them.

The students' participation skills in this classroom progressed during the course of the year. At the outset, they mostly responded to the teacher's initiation acts. Their attempts to initiate were few, and most were ineffective. Some of these initiations were sanctioned by the teacher as out of phase with the lesson. Others did reach the floor, but were left there, unattended by other participants. Once the students learned to recognize the seams in classroom discourse, the raw number of students' initiation acts increased, as did the effectiveness of these acts. Soon, students' initiations were picked up by others, and finally, they influenced the course of lessons.

THE INTERPRETIVE ASPECT OF CLASSROOM PARTICIPA-TION   Because classroom rules are tacit and implicitly communicated, students must engage in active interpretive work. Students interpret implicit classroom rules that specify different courses of action and that vary from occasion to occasion. Successful participation in the culture of the classroom involves the ability to relate behavior, both academic and social, to a given classroom situation in terms of implicit rules. This involves going beyond the information given in verbal instructions to understand the teacher, linking particular features to general patterns by filling in contextual information (compare Cicourel, 1973).

Competent membership in the classroom community, then, involves weaving academic knowledge and interactional skills together like strands of a rope, providing factually correct academic content in the interactionally appropriate form. The separation of form and content leads to inappropriate behavioral displays in the classroom. This is as much the case for the student who provides content without form as it is for the student who provides form without content. The student who knows academic information but does not know how to provide it (for example, has not mastered the procedures for gaining access to the floor, and so bids for the floor when replies are acceptable, or replies when bids have been called for) will be out of phase with classroom interaction, as will the student who knows how to get the floor but does not know what to do with it once he or she has it.

5   CONCLUSIONS

THIS HAS BEEN a look inside an elementary school classroom at teacher-student interaction during classroom lessons. Classroom lessons have been described here as sequentially and hierarchically organized events assembled by the structuring work of teachers interacting with students. A discussion of membership in the classroom community accompanied this analysis of the social organization of classroom lessons. Competent participation in these classroom events was depicted in terms of the integration of academic knowledge and interactional skills.

This constitutive ethnography of classroom lessons is grounded in, and retrievable from, empirical evidence made available by a systematic analysis of transcripts and videotape of naturally occurring classroom events. In addition, the analysis has been faithful to the policies of locating the social organization of these events in the interaction between classroom participants, and demonstrating that this interactional machinery actually guides the classroom participants.

In this final chapter, the specifics of this particular study will be linked to some more general issues. These issues are (1) the nature of findings from constitutive ethnography, (2) the relation of this constitutive ethnography to other studies of classroom interaction, and (3) the consequences of the differences between the organization of talking in classrooms and in everyday life. In the final section of this chapter, I will consider new directives for constitutive ethnographic work.

172

The Nature of Findings from Constitutive Ethnography

In attempting to specify the cultural knowledge that the teacher and students in this classroom used in order to negotiate their interaction together, I have presented a model to describe that interaction. But I am not content to have this be "any" model. I want to insure that it is the model actually used (if not articulated) by the participants as well. In describing the social organization of classroom lessons in such a way that the researcher's model captures the participants' actual practice, the notion of "news" in research is being treated in a unique way. Some sociologists reject the notion that scientific knowledge can be claimed when research reveals "what everybody knows" (Davis, 1971). I do not see the purpose of my analysis to be the presentation of unexpected findings. Instead, I see a major purpose of constitutive ethnography to be the presentation of information that the participants themselves already "know" but may have not been able to articulate. Such ethnography may reveal patterns of interaction that surprise participants or scientists, but surpise is not the criterion of value.

Consider the case of the anthropologist preparing a description of a particular tribal practice in which people dance in a certain way in order to create rain. If that anthropologist's ethnography is done well, members of the tribe will, in effect, nod their heads and shrug their shoulders in a way that suggests, "What else is new?" The members' yawned "of course" is not to be taken as criticism; it is a compliment. It affirms that the researcher has depicted a segment of a people's cultural knowledge in a way that is consistent with their practice.

In research conducted in less exotic settings, such as a classroom, ethnographers strive for that shrugged "of course" as an affirmation of their description. Because they are knowledgeable as members (or former members) of such groups, successful description ought to reveal what they know (after the fact, perhaps) to be so. The "news" in any investigation of members' knowledge does not come from the presentation of startling, counterintuitive findings; it comes from the presentation of findings that resonate with members' own way of proceeding. This is as much the case whether the members' knowledge being explored is linguistic (Chomsky, 1965; Hymes, 1974), cultural (Tyler, 1969), or commonsense (Schutz, 1962; Garfinkel, 1967) knowledge.

Chomsky (1965) is very clear on this point. He says that a linguistic theory is "descriptively adequate to the extent that it correctly describes the intrinsic competence of the idealized native speaker" (p. 24). "There is no way to avoid the traditional assumption that the speaker-hearer's linguistic intuition is the ultimate standard that determines the accuracy of any proposed grammar, linguistic theory, or operational test" (p. 22). He also recognizes that members may not be able to state their knowledge of language in so many words: "It must be emphasized once again that this tacit knowledge will not be immediately available to the user of the language" (p. 22). Although the linguistic description explicates the members' implicit knowledge, this description is not treated as a superior formulation: "In bringing to consciousness the triple ambiguity of . . . [a sentence analyzed by Chomsky] in this way, we present no new information to the hearer and teach him nothing about his language, but simply arrange matters in such a way that his linguistic intuition, previously obscured, becomes evident to him" (p. 22).[1]

Although the domain of inquiry is different, a position consistent with Chomsky's is formulated by Garfinkel (1967). Like Polanyi (1962) and Schutz (1962) before him, Garfinkel attributes a tacit dimension to commonsense knowledge of the social structure: "There is a characteristic disparity between publicly acknowledged determinations and the personal withheld determinations of events, and this private knowledge is held in reserve, i.e., *the event means for both the witness and the other more than the witness can say*" (p. 56; emphasis added). A purpose of this style of inquiry, as of certain linguistic and anthropological studies, is to insure that the researcher's knowledge resonates with the participants' knowledge of the world. They study "is directed to a description of the work by which decisions of meaning and fact are managed . . . *from within the society*" (pp. 76-77).

Like Chomsky, Garfinkel does not suggest that his findings are to be accorded a privileged position or have a superior status: "Ethnomethodological studies are not directed to formulating or arguing correctives. They are useless when they are done as ironies . . . Similarly, there can be nothing to quarrel with or correct about practical sociological reasoning" (p. vii).

A similar position is to be found in a variety of papers collected by Tyler (1969) representing that school of anthropological thought variously called ethnoscience, cognitive anthropology, componential analysis, and ethnographic semantics. Frake (1969:123) presents the point of view that the purpose of ethnography is to describe the cultural knowledge of the members of a society:

> Ethnography according to this image, is a description which seeks to account for the behavior of a people by describing the socially acquired and shared knowledge of a culture that enables members of the society to behave in ways deemed appropriate among themselves . . . Accounting for socially meaningful behavior within a given society is not the sole aim of ethnography. By developing methods for the demonstrably successful description of messages, as manifestations of a code, one is further seeking to build a theory of codes—a theory of culture.

Black and Metzger (1969:140) add, "Investigators in this field generally agree that it is the ethnographer's duty to report the significant dimensions as perceived and reacted to by participants in the culture . . . His resulting analysis is expressed in *their* meaningful units." Frake (1969:124) draws the parallel between the linguistic analysis of members' knowledge and the ethnographic analysis of this knowledge: "First, it is not the ethnographer's task to predict behavior per se, but rather to state the rules of culturally appropriate behavior. In this respect, the ethnographer is akin to the linguist who does not attempt to predict what people will say, but to state the rules for constructing utterances which native speakers will judge as grammatically appropriate." Moerman (1969: 450) contributes the point of view that the researcher's perspective is not superior to the member's knowledge: "To become familiar with a culture is to find no surprises in it and to regard native explanations as analyses instead of data."

The position I have adopted in this study is based on these formulations of the basic ethnographic position. Hence, when it is said that a description of members' knowledge is not unexpected, it is in the sense that the description is not unexpected by the participants because it approximates their cultural knowledge.

In addition to generating a description that approximates the knowledge of participants in a particular event, this method of investigation can also serve as a vocabulary for participants themselves to articulate their own tacit knowledge, thereby making the implicit explicit, the invisible visible. Put into practice, this would be a concrete example of Hymes's (1972:xxxvi) recommendation that educators become "ethnographers of their own situation."

THE CORROBORATION OF FINDINGS   While the work reported here may be taken as an adequate description of interaction during lesson time in one classroom, questions about the corroboration of these findings in other classrooms remain. Can other researchers locate the same structures and structurings we have found when they examine this corpus of materials? Will a similar model of interaction be found in other classrooms? Or in the same classroom when lessons are conducted in a different format or by a different teacher?

The first question addresses the issue of the reproducibility of findings, while the second addresses the issue of the generalizability of findings.

Reproducibility.   The issue of reproducibility of findings is usually addressed obliquely in social science research, expressed in terms of "coder reliability." Under this rubric, research assistants are trained to score answers to survey questions or experimentally induced behavior in accordance with a certain coding scheme. Reliability is said to be achieved when separate coders independently assign similar behavior to similar categories. While this approach insures that coders are socialized into the researcher's way of seeing the world, the researcher's model is not examined directly; it remains a part of the implicit background informing the interpretive enterprise.

Because the corpus of materials for this study, and other constitutive ethnographies, is preserved on videotape, the issue of reproducibility can be addressed more directly. I would imagine that the test of reproducibility would proceed in the following way. An independent investigator would be presented with this description of the lessons on the one hand, and the corpus of materials on the other. The description would serve as "instructions for looking." It would be that independent investigator's task to try and reproduce the same model of interaction described in this report. The extent to which he was successful would indicate the extent to which this is not a private model but a publicly verifiable one (compare McDermott, Gospodinoff, and Aron, 1978).

Generalizability. When the issue of generalizability of findings has been considered in social science research, it also has been in statistical terms. Just as reproducibility is defined in terms of a certain percentage of coder reliability, so, too, generalizability is said to be obtained when a statistical correlation of a certain magnitude is obtained between the findings in one setting and the findings in another setting.

This method would not be used with constitutive studies. The phenomena in constitutive ethnography are structural, not statistical. Therefore, the concern is whether the structural arrangements located in this classroom will be recapitulated in other classrooms, or even in other kinds of interactional events.

The structural arrangements located here are sequential and hierarchical. The sequential structure, in turn, has been described as the organization of teacher-student behavior into interactional sequences. While I did report the percentage of interactional sequences initiated by teachers and students (table 2.3), the percentage of types of initiation acts (table 2.2), and the percentage of three-part and extended sequences (table 2.2), those statistical arrays are not the essential points for comparison.

The more crucial issues are the structural arrangements

themselves. As you remember, teacher and student actions did not occur randomly or haphazardly in these lessons. They occurred in particular patterns and in a particular order. For example, neither the students nor the teacher initiated a new round of interaction with an evaluation of past performance or a reply. Only new information occurred in the first slot of a sequence. Likewise, teacher and student behavior occurred in a particular order. For example, students raised their hands after the teacher invited bids for the floor, replied after the teacher elicited information, sharpened pencils after the teacher gave directives. That is, teacher-student behavior was organized into interactional sequences that had initiation-reply-evaluation components. Furthermore, a very strong co-occurrence relationship was found between initiations and replies, such that types of initiations and types of replies were tied together, and symmetrical initiation-reply pairs were invariably followed by an evaluation marking that symmetry. A similar co-occurrence relationship was found between the initiators of action and respondents of action. The respondent identified as part of an initiation act provided the next reply. Participants reacted to deviations from this pattern by repairing broken symmetries.

When the generalizability of these findings is tested, the recurrence of those tying structures will be investigated. An issue like the following will be considered: do classroom events other than lessons, or events in other classrooms, give evidence of tying structures among initiation-reply-evaluation acts and initiators and respondents?

The teacher evaluated the completion of initiation-reply sequences with a positive comment (like "good"), often while repeating a student's reply. While I would not necessarily expect the exact vocabulary of this classroom to be duplicated (another teacher might nod or say "fine"), I would predict that equivalent structural arrangements would be duplicated. Lessons in other classrooms and other classroom events would be found to have a sequential structure that would be marked in some recurrent, readily recognizable way.

The same approach would be repeated regarding hierarchical arrangements. Interactional sequences are arranged into higher-order lesson components called phases, and phases, in turn, assemble the event called the lesson. Particular sequences perform particular functions, and so occur in different phases of lessons. Directives and informatives compose the opening and closing phases of lessons, while elicitations make up the major activity in the instructional phase of lessons. Each of these hierarchical components is marked by the participants' actions.

When these findings are compared to other classroom events and to other classrooms, the recurrence of these structural arrangements will be under review. Again, I would not necessarily expect to see the teacher and students in some other classroom exercise exactly the same options for demonstrating their orientation to hierarchical components, but I would expect to see other classroom events recapitulating a hierarchical structure. Indeed, evidence is accumulating to that effect. Bremme and Erickson (1977); Erickson and Shultz (1978); Florio (1978); McDermott (1976); McDermott, Gospodinoff, and Aron (1978); Shultz (1976); and Shuy and Griffin (1978) have already reported similar structural arrangements in counseling sessions, reading groups, and classroom discussion sessions.

I have emphasized that the structure of classroom lessons is assembled by the joint interactional activity of teachers and students. Most notably in this regard, the teacher and students participated in a turn-allocation machinery to maintain order in this classroom. Basic turn-allocation procedures and improvisational strategies did the work of maintaining classroom lessons as socially organized events.

I imagine that other classroom events in other classrooms will be found to be ordered by similar structuring work. I base this prediction on evidence accumulating in parallel studies of the classroom (Bremme and Erickson, 1977; McDermott, 1976; Shultz, 1976), and in similar studies of social organization in medical (Sudnow, 1965; Garfinkel, 1967:187-206; Scheflen, 1972), legal (Cicourel, 1968), scientific, and "nonordinary" settings (for a review, see Mehan and Wood, 1975, 1976). Taken together, this group of studies shows that the "objective social facts" of a setting are a collaborative production of the participants involved.

So, in one sense, although no formal comparison of this model of teacher-student interaction has been made, informal evidence of the generalizability of these findings is already accumulating. More self-conscious comparisons will concentrate on structural features, not statistical arrays, with the expectation that basic structural arrangements will be recapitulated reflexively in functionally equivalent ways. That is, events will be found to be organized both sequentially and hierarchically; people will be found to be doing the work of organizing events collaboratively. When the work from this project is combined with that of the CAL, Harvard, and Rockefeller groups,[2] we begin to see the fulfillment of a promise of "a new direction" for studies of education (Karabel and Halsey, 1976)—away from positivistic versions of structural functionalism that rely exclusively on input-output models, toward close ethnographic descriptions of the internal life of schools within an interpretive framework.

A Comparison of Approaches to Classroom Interaction

I will now point out how this constitutive ethnographic approach is related to previous approaches to the study of teacher-student interaction. In this section, a discussion of the relationship of language to context, the basis of meaning in discourse, the hierarchical aspects of lesson discourse, the nature of co-occurrence relationships, and the relationship of language form to language function will be presented in order to serve two purposes simultaneously. First, the topics will be used to show how this study has been influenced by the "product-process" approach (Dunkin and Biddle, 1974; Brophy and Good, 1974), work in the "information-exchange" tradition (notably Bloom et al., 1956; Guilford, 1956), and previous discourse analysis in the classroom (Bellack et al., 1966; Sinclair and Coulthard, 1975). Second, these topics will be used to draw out the differences between this previous work and the approaches developed here.

THE CONTEXTUAL BASIS OF LANGUAGE   I tried to build on previous field and quantitative studies of the classroom, but, as explained in chapter 1, I found that such studies were either too global or too fragmentary. In describing how constitutive or microethnographic studies differ from participant-observation and quantitative approaches to the study of classroom interaction, I explained that some researchers, especially those in the participant-observation tradition, quote large sections of field notes or conversations and make a few summary statements about them, while schemes like that of Flanders (Amidon and Flanders, 1963; Flanders, 1970) extract particular elements of the interaction ("accepts feelings," "accepts ideas," "asks questions") in unpredictable ways.

The same can be said for the "process-product" approach to classroom interaction. The studies summarized in Dunkin and Biddle (1974) extract indices of teachers' instructional style, classroom organization, and the like from the classroom context. These become "process measures," which are linked with educational test results and other "product measures." Arithmetic operations are then performed on the indices. These tabulations may show some long-range trends, but they are far removed from the machinery generating and governing discourse and interaction in the classroom, and they have little value to practitioners.

Interaction in classrooms does not occur in isolated acts of teacher and student talk. It occurs in connected discourse, situated in a social context. In a charming example of a language game involving a teacher and an apprentice, Wittgenstein (1952) provides persuasive evidence for the need to place discourse in context. He demonstrates that every act of speaking and pointing is inherently ambiguous. As a result, the meaning of words is not decided without knowledge of context in which language is used.

Many current investigators, some clearly influenced by Wittgenstein, have drawn similar conclusions about the limitations of extracting particular elements of interaction from their context. Garfinkel (1967:39), for example, concludes his discussion of attempts to interpret a brief conversation between a husband and a wife by saying, "there were many matters that . . . partners understood they were talking about that they did not mention . . . [and] many matters that partners understood were understood on the basis not only of what was actually said, but what was left unspoken." That is, all the information that conversationalists need in order to understand each other is not located in the linguistic utterances exchanged between them. Because of the sketchiness and vagueness of spoken utterances, conversationalists must "look elsewhere than what was said in order to find the corresponding contents" (Garfinkel, 1967:40). They must attend to contextually provided features, which include knowledge of "the biography and purposes of the speaker, the circumstances of the utterances, the previous course of conversation, or the particular relationship of actual or potential interaction which exists between user and auditor" (ibid.). Findings such as these recommend that language abstracted from daily use be abandoned in favor of the study of language in its social context, a position that Hymes (1974), Labov (1972), and Shuy, Wolfram, and Riley (1967) have been most vocal in advocating.

The treatment of classroom lessons as contextually based discourse reinforces the view that language is interactional. Lessons are organized into units of increasing size and complexity, from three-part sequences to phases, each of which is produced jointly by teachers and students. Classroom lessons and other forms of discourse have a different ontological status than utterances or sentences. While people *produce* sentences or utterances, people *participate* in discourse. While the presence of a sentence as a thing-in-the-world requires only one speaker, the presence of a lesson or other form of discourse requires participants. Discourse is social activity, larger, more encompassing than any of the parties involved. It is a prime example of what Durkheim (1896) meant when he talked about the existence of a distinctive social reality, a reality *sui generis*.

The treatment of classroom lessons as contextually based discourse has the further consequence of transforming the conception of academic instruction. By reinforcing the idea that instruction is participatory in nature, not solitary behavior, instruction is removed from a psychological or a personal plane and is placed on a social or an interpersonal plane.

THE BASIS OF MEANING IN DISCOURSE I did find the work of Bellack and his colleagues (1966) and Sinclair and Coulthard (1975) helpful in many respects. By using the notion of "language games," Bellack demonstrated the utility of Wittgenstein's (1952) approach to language use for the study of language in naturally occurring situations. Sinclair and Coulthard were among the first to apply speech-act theory systematically to the study of discourse in an institutional setting. The major speech acts they identified in the classroom served as conceptual heuristics for this study. Sinclair and Coulthard's "feedback," and Bellack's "reacting move" were especially helpful, as they forced me to rethink the entire issue of reflexive tying in discourse and led me to characterize the sequential organization of classroom discourse as variations of ordered triples instead of as the adjacency pairs associated with everyday discourse.

There are considerable differences between these previous treatments of classroom discourse and the treatment here, however. I identified directives, informatives, and elicitations as the major constituents of lessons, as did Sinclair and Coulthard. However, my reasons for making that distinction differ from those of Sinclair and Coulthard significantly. Sinclair and Coulthard rely heavily on grammatical features and distinctions between channels of communications, while I identify the function of speech in discourse reflexively. For example, they distinguish between directives and elicitations based on the modality of the response. Their elicitation is defined as a request for a verbal response, and their directive is defined as a request for a nonverbal action. I did not find the distinction between verbal and nonverbal heuristic. Many teacher elicitations in the lessons require students to demonstrate their reasoning by nonverbal means, for example, by pointing to names on a chart (see the Namecards lesson, Mehan et al., 1976), or by picking up cards from the floor (see the S and J Words lesson). Therefore, I distinguish between directives and elicitations based on the function of the action demanded, as determined by subsequent action. Elicitations exchange academic information, both verbally and nonverbally. Directives are requests for procedural actions such as sharpening pencils or arranging chairs (see Mehan et al., 1976:216-22).

The Sinclair and Coulthard method of classifying elicitation sequences involves identifying the head of the sequence. They begin with the grammatical classification of an utterance and, if necessary, add information about the situation. They then apply sorting rules to make fine distinctions, for example, between rhetorical questions and real questions. As was explained in chapter 2, I found that grammatically based categories could not be applied to my materials to determine what was happening between teacher and students in lessons.

I found that the same problem limited the utility of typologies of classroom interaction in the "process-product" tradition. After identifying the major initiation acts in classroom discourse, I attempted to further specify the cognitive demands of the acts in the elicitation class of initiation acts. As described in chapter 2, I settled on choice, product, process, and metaprocess elicitations. This index of elicitations is comparable to and influenced by other typologies of classroom information exchange.

My "choice elicitation" is similar to Brophy and Good's (1974:90) "choice questions." These types of acts specify that the respondent chooses answers from among a list provided by the initiator. The "product elicitation" asks respondents to provide a factual response such as names, places, dates, or colors. It is similar to Bloom et al.'s (1956) "knowledge," Guilford's (1956) "cognition" and "memory," and Brophy and Good's (1974:90) "product question." Each of these concepts is defined as a demand for factual information from the respondent based on the cognitive processes of recall, recognition, or rote recitation. The "process elicitation" asks for students' opinions or interpretations. It is similar to Bloom et al.'s "skills and abilities," Guilford's "evaluation" and "explanation," and Brophy and Good's "process" and "opinion" questions. Bloom says "skills" require a student to apply a generalized technique but the application does not require special knowledge. "Abilities" require both the recall of factual knowledge and the application of this knowledge to new situations. Guilford's "explanation" is the substantiation of a claim or conclusion by citing evidence. His "evaluation" deals with matters of values rather than matters of fact. Brophy and Good's "process question" requires the student to give detailed explanation or to explain the problem that underlies the answer. Their "opinion" question requires students to make a prediction or evaluate some material.

However, each of these schemes employed the concept of "question." That expression implies that the intention of the speaker or the meaning of an utterance is conveyed by grammatical distinctions: rising intonation, *wh* forms, subject-verb reversal, and so on. Quite simply, I found that the meaning that action had for classroom participants was not conveyed by grammatical means. As explained in chapter 2, I found that the teacher obtained "answers" from students by using forms of speech that would not normally be classified as questions. For example, the teacher might obtain academic information by using a "command": "Go to the board and point to the right one" (Map Words lesson). As a result, I reformulated the unit of analysis from autonomous speech acts to interactionally accomplished sequences of action and allowed the participants' prospective and retrospective treatment of action to decide meaning.

CONCEPTIONS OF HIERARCHICAL ARRANGEMENTS   Like Bellack and his colleagues (1966) and Sinclair and Coulthard (1975), I have characterized lessons as hierarchically organized. However, the sense of hierarchy is considerably different in my scheme than in these other schemes.[4] Their sense of hierarchy is one of a rank scale of units. A unit at a given rank is made up of one or more units of the rank below and combines with units of the same rank to make up a unit at the rank above. This "nesting" of units enables Sinclair and Coulthard to talk about the lesson as composed of a set of transactions, which in turn are composed of a set of teacher-student exchanges. As Griffin and Humphrey (1978) point out, rank-scale units are abstractions from the data. They are analyst's constructs, which are not necessarily meaningful units for the participants. Furthermore, not every unit in the hierarchy is available to be seen in the interaction between the participants. I follow Sacks (1963), and agree with Griffin and Humphrey (1978), in saying that units of analysis that are not identifiable from surface features are not admissible as analytic devices. Each level of my hierarchical scheme—interactional sequences, topically related sets, and phases—is grounded in the data.

Furthermore, I am able to show that the students learned the structure of lessons while participating in them. The children in this classroom became more effective in responding appropriately (in timing and form) as well as correctly (in content) as the year progressed. Since none of the participants, not even the teacher, knew the structure of lessons explicitly, the students were learning more than anyone could have explicitly taught them. Because I can show that my hierarchical units are available in the behavior of the participants and are learned by them in the course of their interaction together, I have a stronger warrant for claiming that they are pragmatically meaningful to the participants as well as descriptively useful for the researcher.

CONCEPTIONS OF CO-OCCURENCE   There is a "weak" sense of co-occurrence operating in the schemes of Bellack and his colleagues (1966) and Sinclair and Coulthard (1975), and a "strong" sense of co-occurrence or reflexive tying in our system. The weak sense of co-occurrence in the former systems predicts possible combinations of teacher and student acts that simply do not occur in the data (Griffin and Humphrey, 1978). Bellack and his colleagues and Sinclair and Coulthard allow any combination of initiation, reply, and evaluation acts from complete nonoccurrence to complete presence. As Griffin and Humphrey graphically demonstrate, this is not the way that classroom discourse is organized. Evaluations do not just occur in isolation, before, during, or in the middle of an initiation-reply sequence. Likewise, replies do not occur in isolation or without an initiation act. Each of these acts occurs in specific slots in discourse, and participants are quick to note the "official absence" of behavior from these conversational slots.

A strong sense of co-occurrence or reflexive tying enables us to make predictions about the overall organization of lessons, including the relationship between constituent components of sequences and the relationship of sequences to lesson phases. We are saying that teacher and student behavior occurs in obligatory relationships. For example, certain acts in the reply frame are demanded by certain acts in the initiation frame, and this relationship in turn establishes an obligatory relationship with certain kinds of evaluation acts. Thus, a sequence in which an evaluation act does not appear immediately after an initiation-reply pair is not just another statistical category. It signals that something important is happening in the interaction: teacher and students are engaging in recovery or repair work to recalibrate the interactional machinery of lessons via extended sequences (see chapter 2), improvisational strategies, (see chapter 3), or accomplished evaluations (see Griffin and Humphrey, 1978). The presence of this recovery work in the absence of normatively produced action provided by a strong sense of flexive tying establishes a strong warrant for claims about the reality of the analysis for the participants.

FORM AND FUNCTION IN LANGUAGE   Yet another difference between the approach to discourse taken by Bellack and his colleagues (1966) and Sinclair and Coulthard (1975) on the one hand, and this constitutive ethnographic approach on the other, concerns the relationship between language form and the functions of language.

The traditional view of language is that it serves a "referential" function (Sebeok, 1962:434). According to this view, the purpose of language is to describe things. Accordingly, words stand for referents, pointing to or indicating objects in the world.

While making connections between signs and objects in

the world may be a primary purpose of language, this is not the only function that language performs. Austin (1962), for example, showed that people do many things with their words besides refer to objects. Most notably, he pointed out that words perform deeds. That is, there are certain classes of actions, like apologizing, promising, pledging, that are accomplished by the very act of speaking words. For example, the saying of the words, "I am sorry," constitutes an apology.

Furthermore, while communicating, a person is not only transferring information about a referent. He or she is conveying information about his or her very existence and about the relationship between the parties, and is commenting on language itself. Moreover, these "affective" and "metacommunicative" (Sebeok, 1962) functions are not only communicated verbally. The work of Birdwhistell (1970), Kendon (1970), and Scheflen (1972) is especially instructive on this point, for it shows that the ways in which words are spoken, involving such features as voice set, voice quality, stress, pitch, the spacing and timing between words, combined with postural configurations and body movement, can communicate the emotional state of the person speaking, comment on the relationship between speaker and hearer, or inform others about how words are to be interpreted. The "ums," "ahs," "uh huhs," eye contact, glances, head nods, and other "back channel" work discussed by Duncan (1972) are further examples of this metacommunicative activity, which serves to establish, prolong, or discontinue communication and seems to accompany talk about referents.

These investigations suggest that language serves many and diverse functions. In so doing, they move well away from what Wittgenstein (1952) called "nomenclature" theories of language, which seem to say that language serves a single, referential function. While alerting us to the multiple functions of language, these investigators seem to operate on the implicit assumption that any single speech form can serve only one function at a time. While language in general can serve a denotative, an affective, or a metacommunicative function, a particular act of speech cannot serve more than one function at a time. Different functions are assigned to different aspects of the message, or to different channels of the communicative process. So, for example, facial expressions and tone of voice are said to convey emotion, while denotative meaning is conveyed linguistically and carried in the verbal channel.

Many discourse analysts adopt a version of this single-form-single-function position. It is particularly evident in the Sinclair and Coulthard (1975) treatment of speaker selection. The selection of the next speaker is but one of many possible initiation acts for Sinclair and Coulthard (compare Brophy and Good, 1974). By contrast, I have adopted a position that maintains that a single speech form can serve more than one language function at a time. For example, I build speaker selection into each teacher-student sequence because I have found that each initiation act both announces the action to be taken and identifies the population of people who are to take the action.

There are many further examples of interaction in this corpus of data (see Streeck, 1978 for an extended analysis) and in other studies (Labov and Fanschel, 1977; Shuy and Griffin, 1978) that give evidence that a single speech form can serve more than one language function at a time. The teacher's sanction of a student's action can serve a retrospective and a prospective function simultaneously. Retrospectively, the teacher's sanction serves as an evaluation of an inappropriate action that has occurred in the past; prospectively, it serves as a statement of expectation for future actions. In a similar manner, a teacher's comment on the content of one student's reply can serve an evaluative function while simultaneously serving an initiation function for the next speaker. And inversely, the teacher's selection of the next student in a round of reading simultaneously accomplishes the evaluation of the previous reader's work (Griffin and Humphrey, 1978).

The possibility that a single linguistic or communicative form can perform multiple functions simultaneously has profound implications for schemes of analysis that attempt to code behavior into discrete, mutually exclusive categories. If this possibility becomes a general finding, it will challenge us to rethink simple, discrete, linear models of analysis, and will invite us to consider models that are unitary, interconnected, and reflexive.

Conversation in the Classroom and in Everyday Life

It seems important to compare the organization of interaction in classroom events with the organization of interaction in other interactional encounters, especially those that transpire outside of the classroom, as a means of understanding the relations between schooling and society at large.

There are many important points of similarity between discourse in lessons and discourse in everyday life. First of all, a classroom lesson is an everyday situation of interaction in which people address each other for a period of time, communicating something about themselves and their knowledge of certain academic matters in the process. In this sense, classroom lessons are a member of the family of "speech events" (Hymes, 1974): routinized forms of behavior, delineated by well-defined boundaries and well-defined sets of behavior within those boundaries.

Classroom lessons, like other speech events, are interactional accomplishments, dependent upon participation by many parties for the assembly of their structure. Classroom lessons, like other interactionally accomplished events, have a sequential organization in which talking shifts from party to party as the event unfolds. Classroom lessons, like other interactional events, have a hierarchical organization marked by recurrent behavioral configurations. In lessons, as in other polite speech events, speakers take turns, overlapping utterances are not highly valued, and access to the floor is obtained in systematic ways.

Despite these similarities fostered by the resemblance among members of the family of speech events, there is not a one-to-one correspondence between conversation in everyday life and conversation in classrooms. These points of contrast, and their educational consequences will be discussed in this section.

TURN TAKING IN CLASSROOM INTERACTION AND IN EVERYDAY INTERACTION   There are interesting points of comparison between turn taking in speech events that occur in the classroom and in speech events that occur in other social situations. Sacks, Schegloff, and Jefferson (1974) array kinds of talk along a continuum according to how turns are allocated. Debates anchor one end of this continuum because turns there are allocated in advance. Conversations are at the other end because turns there are allocated "locally," that is, during the course of talk. Classroom lessons can be said to be a kind of speech event that falls along this continuum because of the way in which these turn-taking options are transformed into turn-allocation procedures.

Sacks, Schegloff, and Jefferson (1974) say that the turn-taking mechanism for normal conversation insures that (1) one party speaks at a time, (2) speaker change recurs, and (3) conversation is accomplished with precise timing ("no gaps and no overlaps"). Each speaker when allocated a turn has an initial right to speak. The end of a turn signals the possible transition place between speakers. The transfer of turns from one speaker to another properly occurs at that juncture.

According to Sacks and his colleagues, the specific mechanism for speaker allocation is accomplished by an ordered set of rules, which is applied recursively to generate the distribution of turns for any actual conversation. At any possible juncture, the current speaker can select the next speaker. If the current-speaker does not exercise this option, other potential speakers can select themselves to be next speaker. In the absence of "current speaker selects next speaker" and "next speaker selects self" options, the current speaker can select him or herself and continue speaking.

These three options are not exercised in equivalent ways during classroom lessons. Turn allocation in these lessons is almost exclusively of the "current speaker selects next speaker" type. In fact, the individual nomination, invitation to bid, and invitation to reply procedures can be seen as specific practices by which the teacher, as current speaker, selects the students as next speaker. The participants' almost exclusive reliance on this particular turn-allocation practice maintains lesson control in the teacher's hands. This choice helps her actualize her utilitarian concern for order in the classroom. The predominance of this procedure over the others marks a significant difference between classroom conversation and normal conversation.

Everyday conversation is devoid of many of the features associated with classroom conversation. The invitation to bid and invitation to reply procedures simply do not occur in everyday conversation. If "recyclable" and "automatic" turn allocation occur at all in everyday conversation, their density and duration are certainly limited (Griffin and Humphrey, 1978).

Yet another difference between everyday conversation and classroom conversation concerns turn-change junctures. In the characterization of everyday conversation by Sacks, Schegloff, and Jefferson (1974), conversation is a free-ranging speech event between (at least) two parties. Each party has the opportunity to determine the direction of discourse and to a certain extent influences successive topics. This implies that speaker allocation is open for negotiation at the end of each turn in everyday conversation. This is not the case for conversation in classrooms. Speakers in lessons cannot take the floor at the end of every turn as they can in everyday conversation. There are special junctures for speaker change. The floor is open for negotiation only at certain junctures, namely at the end of an initiation-reply-evaluation sequence or at the completion of a topically related set of sequences.

Furthermore, the teacher not only allocates the floor; she takes it back at the end of a student's reply. While there are instances of students evaluating each other's replies (8:113, 8:117, 9:45, 9:46) and following one another as next initiator (scattered examples in CIS #8, #9) we do not see students directly selecting the next speaker during their reply to a teacher's initiation. A sequence like the following[3] simply does not occur during these lessons.

Initiation	Reply	Evaluation
T: Where is the red flower, Richard?	R: Under the tree?	
R: What do you think Cindy?	C: I guess you're right.	

The overwhelming presence of sequences in which the teacher selects next speakers to the exclusion of sequences where students select next speakers is another difference between conversation in lessons and conversations in everyday life that can be seen in the interaction.

This is not to say that the selection of students to be next speaker by students never occurs in the classroom. During classroom events other than lessons, such as "show and tell time," students may select other students during their turns of talk. We must take care not to characterize the overall structure of interaction in classrooms based on the organization of one particular classroom event, namely lessons. Instead of overgeneralizing, we need to systematically describe interaction in the array of events that routinely occur in educational and other institutional settings. When such descriptions are assembled, we will have an empirical rather than a speculative basis for distinguishing among kinds of speech events.

SEQUENTIAL FEATURES OF CLASSROOM CONVERSATION AND EVERYDAY CONVERSATION   Another way to characterize the difference between classroom conversation and everyday conversation is in terms of sequential organization. Although classroom lessons are like other interactional events in that talking shifts from party to party as the event unfolds, there are differences in the internal organization of that sequencing.

Polite conversations (Sacks, Schegloff, and Jefferson, 1974) and some other speech events (such as therapeutic interviews—see Labov and Fanschel, 1977) have been characterized as having a two-part sequential structure. The speech of one party is coupled reflexively to the speech of another party. The conversation is built up of adjacency pairs—summonses are tied to answers, greetings to greetings, questions to answers—from its beginning to its end.

The basic pattern of sequential organization in classroom lessons seems to be an interactional sequence composed of three, not two, reflexively linked parts (see chapter 2; compare Shuy and Griffin, 1978). The following hypothetical example is typical of the initiation-reply-evaluation pattern:

Speaker A: "What time is it, Denise?" Speaker B: "Two-thirty." Speaker A: "Very good, Denise." The presence of the evaluation slot, which comments on the completion of the immediately preceding initiation-reply pair, seems to be a distinguishing feature of classroom conversation.

This is not to say that a three-part sequence with evaluation as the third constituent is a special province of the classroom. A play rehearsal is another place where the evaluation of a previous reply could be heard. There are also times when three-part sequences occur in everyday conversations (compare Sinclair and Coulthard, 1975:37): Speaker A: "What time is it, Denise?" Speaker B: "Two-thirty." Speaker A: "Thank you, Denise."

Although each of the preceding examples has a three-part sequential structure, the third component does not seem to serve the same function in the second example as in the first example. While "very good, Denise" clearly evaluates the content of the previous reply, "thank you, Denise" does not seem to do this. It seems to be more an acknowledgment of the previous reply than an evaluation of it.

One explanation that can be made for the ubiquitous presence of evaluation in the third slot of interactional sequences in the classroom is the special function of education. It is said to be the teacher's responsibility in his or her role as educator to evaluate the quality of the student's performance (Bellack et al., 1966; Dreeben, 1968; Jackson, 1968; Sinclair and Coulthard, 1975:36-37; Dunkin and Biddle, 1974). Becker and associates (as quoted by Doyle, 1978) depict this position: "The formal structure of classroom tasks can be defined as an exchange of performance for grades."

Another way to account for the unique three-part sequence with its evaluative constituent is to distinguish between elicitations in which the asker already has information and hence has no immediate need for information, and elicitations in which the asker does not have information and hence has an immediate need for information. The former have been called by many names, including "requests for display" or "test questions" (Labov and Fanschel, 1977:89), "information probing questions" (Levin, 1977), and "known-information questions" (Shuy and Griffin, 1978). The latter have been called "requests for information" (Labov and Fanschel, 1978:89), "information-seeking questions" (Levin, 1977), and simply "real questions" (Searle, 1969:69).

When known-information questions are in use, the initiator of the elicitation already has the information, or at least has established the parameters in which a reply can properly fall, and is testing the knowledge of others. The respondent is placed in the position of matching the initiator's predetermined knowledge, or at least of falling within preestablished parameters. When information-seeking questions, or "real" questions, are in use, the initiator does not have the information, the respondent does. The initator is genuinely attempting to obtain this information from the respondent.

This distinction is shown in the contrasting presence of acknowledgments and evaluations in the third slot of the sequence. It also accounts for the fact that avoidance is a normatively acceptable reply to known-information questions but not to information-seeking questions. The question, "What is 1/15 of 87?" asked by a teacher can be appropriately answered by a student, "The improper fractions assignment isn't due until tomorrow." In everyday conversation, however, such an action in the face of an information-seeking question would be treated as bizarre (Levin, 1977:112). Thus, with information-seeking elicitations, the emphasis is on the information requested, while with known-information elicitations, the concern is the state of the knower's knowledge (Searle, 1969; Levin, 1977; Labov and Fanschel, 1977; Shuy and Griffin, 1978).

CONSEQUENCES FOR CHILDREN AND FOR CLASSROOM ORGANIZATION The preceding discussion sheds light on some of what students need to learn in order to participate in that ubiquitous classroom event called the lesson. We have seen that some, but not all, of the tacit features that operate between teachers and students during lessons are those that students encounter in everyday conversations. These differences between interaction in events inside and outside of the classroom reminds us that the academic aspect of schooling is enmeshed in a normative web. The fact that there is not a one-to-one correspondence between everyday conversation and classroom conversation has educational consequences for children and for classroom organization.

Between the ages of eighteen months and four years, the child learns the basic rules of syntax (Cazden, 1972:29-56). The child also learns some of the rules of language *use* during this time. Even before children learn to pronounce individual words, they seem to engage in the sequencing activity associated with conversation (Lewis and Rosenblum, 1977). The essays collected by Ervin-Tripp and Mitchell-Kernan (1977) and by Lewis and Rosenblum (1977) show that in the years before entering school the child learns to take a turn at talk, to make a request for action, to modify speech acts to meet the needs of different audiences, and to make social differentiation in address terms, pronouns, and directives.

The developing literature on children's discourse makes it clear that children come to school with considerable knowledge of general conversational rules. However, students need to distinguish the special features of classroom talk from talk in everyday life. Like strangers coming to a new community (Schutz, 1962:91-106), students entering the classroom for the first time must be socialized to new customs. As a result of the differences between interaction in classrooms and interaction in other situations, it is incumbent upon students to keep the special normative demands of the classroom separate and distinct from those of other situations when they engage in classroom interaction.

This is not to say that children must, of necessity, conform to existing classroom structures in order to suceed in school. Although that position is the underlying assumption of assimilationist and deprivationist views of education, it is not the only conclusion to be drawn from this discussion. Here I have in mind the models of education envisioned and enacted for children who come to school with ways of speaking that are different than the presumed standard (students who speak a foreign language or a variant of standard English), or who come to school with ways of acting that are different from the presumed standard. A prevailing approach to this situation has been to change the child. That is, the child is expected to modify his or her speech patterns and social practices to conform to the standards of the classroom. This means, in many cases, that children must leave ideas, ways of speaking, and ways of acting learned at home and with peers behind when they enter the classroom.

When it is recognized that there are a multitude of language varieties, and of social ways of acting, and when it is further recognized that there is a disparity or discontinuity between ways of speaking at home or on the street and ways of acting in the school, it is not necessary to demand that students change to conform to existing classroom organization. The opposite possibility is equally viable: change the classroom to accommodate the child, including a plurality to speech styles and ways of acting.

As far as academic matters are concerned, this "pluralistic" approach means a flexibility of classroom organization, such that individuals or small groups of students with similar learning styles, timing, and interests are provided instruction in ways that meet their needs. Pluralistic arrangements for language in the classroom are endorsed by this conception. Bilingual models, in which students first utilize their home language for the development of language skills and then transfer to classroom language after achieving mastery in the home language, are obvious examples of this pluralistic conception of education.

A similar recommendation follows concerning ways of acting in the school. Instead of demanding that students leave their culture and language in the clothes closet with their jacket and hats, it is possible for teachers to utilize the ideas, activities, and talk that excite students as a way of organizing curriculum. This is not a belated call for "open" (in the sense of free and unstructured) education. What I have in mind entails implementing what Bruner and others have said about "starting instruction with the world of the child" to build toward conceptual mastery and symbolic representation. Examples of how to do this on a practical basis abound. Stories dictated by children about their personal experiences have been used to construct reading programs. Playground feats of strength have been transformed into graphing and measurement operations. Objects (including trash) collected on the way to school have become material for categorization operations. Children's perceptions and questions about each other have served to facilitate discussions of familial and cultural differences.

Scholastic achievement and conceptual mastery are goals that are espoused eloquently and regularly by educators but that are not achieved equally by children who come to school from culturally different backgrounds or who speak alternative forms of English. The reason for this disparity is not a deficiency, neither genetic (Jensen, 1969), nor cultural (Bereiter and Englemann, 1972), on the part of the student. It is a failure of the existing structure of the school to respond to the cultural, linguistic, and cognitive differences among students who come to school to learn lessons about past accomplishments and future possibilities. Although I obviously cannot demonstrate conclusively that a pluralistic approach to education will succeed where previous approaches have failed, I hope that it will be given the same chance to succeed as previous models.

Directions for Classroom Interaction Research

There seems to be a time-honored tradition in academic writing to conclude a book or article with speculations about future research. Such discussions are often places where authors suggest that others do what they wish they had been able to do in the study being reported. Even though the analysis I have presented relied considerably on the notion of rule violations, I will not become an exception to the "speculation rule" here.

What is next for constitutive ethnographic or microethnographic research in education? I would like to suggest that it is important for this line of research to continue to make linkages between social interaction and social structure. Because the locus of this line of research is education, we cannot be content to provide only abstracted formalizations about the structure of interaction. We incur an obligation to link our descriptions of interaction in educational contexts to structural issues concerning the purposes and consequences of education.

I think that a fruitful way to proceed in this direction would be through a comparative or contrastive analysis. This contrast could take many forms, including the comparison of the way in which interaction (especially teaching-learning interaction) is organized in different environments (from different contexts within a classroom or school to comparisons of teaching in nonschool and other institutional settings).

It is also important that the ethnographic approach continue to make linkages between the research community and the community at large. One way this goal can be reached is through participatory research endeavors.

COMPARATIVE CONTEXTS

Within-classroom contrasts. Much of the research on teaching-learning interaction in schools has been conducted in teacher-centered learning environments. One version of a comparative analysis would investigate the influence of the social organization of different educational environments on children's learning and thinking.

Although a variety of classroom contexts has been studied (whole-group lessons, small-group lessons, procedural meetings), more information is needed on the way in which the social organization of different educational environments within the same classroom and with the same children interacts with the characteristics of individual learners to produce different kinds of academic activities. As I understand it, this is a direction that Cole and his associates (Hall et al., 1977; Cole, Hood, and McDermott, 1978) are taking. Here, the idea is to specify the kinds of academic and social demands that different tasks in different situations make on different children. They plan to examine the influence that whole-group, small-group, and individual tutorials have on children's learning activities. One educational consequence of such an investigation would specify the kind of learning that children achieve in order to identify the learning environments that are the best suited to maximize the development of learning skills in children.

Although many of the classrooms studied by constitutive ethnographers or microethnographers have had learning centers, the primary focus to date has been on classroom situations in which the teacher was present. Since students spend a considerable time away from adults, both in and out of school, it is equally important to understand the processes by which children organize interaction and learn when they are with each other and away from adults. This was an auxiliary focus of this study (Mehan, 1977a), and has been pursued more systematically by Cazden (1977), Cazden et al. (1978), and Shuy and Griffen (1978).

Our attempt to gain access to the child's way of organizing interaction and instruction centered around an "instruction chain." The teacher presented a set of instructions to one particular child as a routine part of the day's activities. That child then presented those instructions and taught the task to his or her work group. Analyses of these peer-teaching situations (Cazden et al., 1978; Mehan, 1977a; Streeck, 1978) show considerable differences in organization of instruction, management of authority, and interpersonal relationships. While teacher-directed lessons are dominated by elicitation of information, peer instruction is characterized by the giving and receiving of information. While the teacher relies on the verbal modality to a great extent, students demonstrate and model their instructions, cooperatively completing tasks together.

This line of investigation is important because it reaffirms the fact that we can learn from the ways in which children organize their lives together. If pursued, this line of investigation will also cause us to cast a critical eye on the models of classroom organization that we automatically demand children conform to, namely teacher-directed, individualized performance, personally competitive. Further investigations of children's modes of organizing behavior may suggest ways to insure that classroom instruction goes with the grain of children's experience instead of against it.

Within-school contrasts. A basic tenet of this study has been that if we want to know whether schools make a difference in people's lives, then we have to look closely at what happens to students inside schools. But it may not be sufficient to confine the analysis to the four walls of the classroom. Much of what affects the life (chances) of the student in school occurs outside the classroom. During the course of their daily lives in schools, students come in contact with teachers, nurses, principals, testers, counselors. Each of these educators makes educational decisions about students.

To this point, constitutive ethnographies have been conducted on a number of classroom events, including lessons, reading groups, circles. There have also been some studies of educational testing situations (Mehan, 1973; Cicourel et al., 1974) and counseling sessions (Erickson, 1975; Erickson and Shultz, 1978). But these events have been treated separately; that is, the same students have not been the focus of study in classroom, testing, and decisionmaking situations.

One way to determine the influence of schooling on students would be to study the processes by which educators make decisions about students' careers as they progress through school. What I have in mind is a "constitutive career study." While we have substantial evidence from these separate studies of counseling sessions, tests, and classroom events that educational outcomes are structured in interaction, we do not yet have information about the treatment of the same students in these different, though interrelated, school situations. It would be informative to follow the same group of students through the maze of the school, conducting a constitutive analysis of their treatment by teachers, testers, and counselors. By linking the study of these encounters together, we would be better able to make informed statements about what does make a difference in students' lives in schools.

School-nonschool contrasts. Much of the research on the teaching-learning process and its consequences has been conducted in school settings. Another important way to determine the consequences of education in people's lives would be to compare the ways in which interaction is accomplished in nonschool environments.

Parents obviously interact with their children at home and in other places; children interact with their peers on playgrounds, streets, and so on. How is the structure of peer interaction organized by comparison with the structure of interaction in the classroom? We have long lists of speculations about such matters, but few contrasts of the organization of discourse and interaction at home, on streets, and in school, where many, or at least some of the participants remain the same, with data that is retrievable and can be analyzed repeatedly.

Many of the speculations concern the limitations of lower-class life styles by contrast with middle-class life styles (see, for example, Bereiter and Englemann, 1972). The line of reasoning that accompanies these speculations is that the failure of the lower-class child in school comes from a mismatch between home and school. The home of the lower-class child is seen as disorganized and unruly; the speech of the lower-class child is seen as illogical and ungrammatical. In short, the mode of life of the lower-class child does not match the mode of life demanded in routine school contexts. The conclusion about educational policy that is reached from these speculations is that the lower-class child must be changed in order to succeed in school.

These speculations are unwarranted because they uncritically assume the universality of the middle-class life style. They commit the classic ethnocentric fallacy of employing the values of one cultural group as a standard for another without inquiring into the way of life of the second group on its own terms. Rather than perpetuate the resocialization of children into the culture of the classroom based on ethnocentrism and speculative evidence, it is essential that we obtain more systematic information about the lives of children outside of school: at play, at home, and in other socially organized activities.

Sociolinguistic research (such as Cazden, John, and Hymes, 1972; Labov, 1972; Hymes, 1974) has been somewhat successful in dispelling misconceptions about the lack of organization of different varieties of English. The developing literature on children's culture, notably discourse

(Ervin-Tripp and Mitchell-Kernan, 1977) and play (Sutton-Smith, 1978), shows the limitations of treating the life of the child as a faulted or incomplete version of the adult world. Researchers in these traditions are uncovering the recurrent patterns of organization of the child's world in its own terms.

Unfortunately, to this point, these investigations of children's play and discourse out of school has taken place independently of the analysis of interaction within schools. It would seem productive to construct an analysis of the organization of interaction between a group of students with teachers in the school context and contrast this with the ways in which the same children organize interaction with peers outside of school.

Hall's program of research is promising in this regard. He is analyzing audiotapes of while and black, lower- and middle-class preschool children in ten different situations at home and school. When completed (for a preliminary report, see Hall et al., 1977), it will provide hard data on the organization of interaction for both lower- and middle-class children in equivalent social contexts. Ethnographic data about the lives of children outside school and the organization of family interaction will, I hope, provide educators with the evidence needed to construct learning environments that are consistent with the needs of children from different cultural backgrounds without cultural imposition or distortion.

Teaching and learning also occur in environments other than the school. Businesses, industries, and especially the military engage in formal training programs for their employees. These nonschool, but highly institutionalized, contexts for learning have not received enough research attention. Knowledge about how businesses prepare executives and how factories train workers by contrast with the ways in which schools educate students would be instructive.

Here, the program of work undertaken by Lave (1977) serves as a model. She is comparing the way master tailors instruct their apprentices on the job with the way teachers instruct students in school in Monrovia, Liberia. Her work sheds light on the nature of learning in an institutionalized learning environment other than the school. In so doing, her work has direct bearing on the effect of education on cognitive development. By comparing schooled and nonschooled populations with respect to their performance on selected cognitive tasks, she will be able to assess the transfer of school-based learning versus the transfer of community-based learning.

PARTICIPATORY RESEARCH   At the completion of a research project, when the data are gathered and analyzed, the issue of the use of research remains. Social science researchers, like their colleagues in the natural sciences, have an implicit obligation to report their findings to the community of scholars in their field. They do so by writing reports, which are presented at conferences or which become articles and books.

Researchers working on issues related to teaching and learning not only have an obligation to make accurate reports to the community of scholars; they incur a commitment to make their work meaningful to the community at large. When this commitment has been met at all in the past, the conventional approach has been one of authority: research is given to the educational community as "findings" or "results" at the conclusion of a project.

I have trouble with this conception of the uses of research for a number of reasons: (1) it treats research as static information, a "thing" to be transferred between people like a package; (2) it separates researchers from the larger community by treating the community as a passive audience, whose role it is to accept the findings of research; (3) the researcher assumes a privileged position vis à vis the larger community because of the presumed superiority of knowledge gathered by scientific methods.

A number of social scientists have pointed out that the bulk of social science research results goes to people in positions of power: governmental agencies and business executives (the latter by virtue of the fact that they sit on the boards of private research foundations and receive final research reports). As an alternative to this relationship between researchers and the powerful, Gouldner (1964) advocated that social science researchers become partisans for the powerless by turning over their research results to the poor and disenfranchised.

I do not think that merely changing the audience who receives research solves the problem. Giving the results of research to the powerless instead of the powerful still treats the other as passive, a recipient of information. Even though the audience changes, research is still being done *about* others, and reported *to* others.

Friere's (1968:67) vision of the ideal relationship between the teacher and the student (which he calls "pedagogic action") invites us to consider an alternative relationship between the research community and the larger community (including parents and educators): "The teacher is no longer merely one who teaches, but one who himself is taught in dialog with the students, who in turn, while being taught, also teach. They become jointly responsible for a process in which they all grow. In this process, arguments based on 'authority' are no longer valid." The assumption here is that people are active subjects, responsible for their actions, not passive objects of received information. By substituting "researchers and educators (or parents)" for "teachers and students" in the above quote, we have a recommendation that researchers act *with* educators and parents in a cooperative manner instead of doing research about or on them.

This perspective places researcher and educator in a dialogue. A dialogue, unlike a lecture (which is based on authority), assumes a parity between participants. The purpose of such a dialogue is not to give information or impose findings: it is to provide participants with ways of looking critically at social circumstances, so that they, themselves, can take action to make changes.

This approach has been explored with classroom teachers. It was a feature of this project. It was an organizing principle of the Erickson group's work (see especially Florio, 1978) and the major study of functional language conducted by the Center for Applied Linguistics (Shuy and Griffin, 1978). In these projects, the classroom teacher was not simply asked to be a subject of a prearranged research project, and then given a list of findings at the end of the study. Instead the teachers participated in the research (and, in the case of this project, initiated it), cooperating in research design, framing questions, analyzing data.

A particularly important aspect in the process of involving participants as ethnographers has been the use of "viewing sessions" (Erickson and Shultz, 1978). Videotape from classroom, educational testing, or counseling sessions is viewed by researchers and participants together. Not only does this procedure provide a method of obtaining participants' perspectives and verifying researchers' interpretations (Cicourel et al., 1974; Erickson and Shultz, 1978), it can lead to research ideas that are collaboratively pursued by researcher and teacher (Florio and Walsh, 1976) or which teachers pursue independently (Shuy and Griffin, 1978).

Viewing sessions also serve as a device to enable participants to "see" the often covert aspects of communication and social organization, variations in language use, and the interactional work that organizes patterns of classroom behavior. This is perhaps the most important aspect of the participatory aspect of the ethnographic perspective, for if people in a particular situation are blind to its nature, then the researcher can not see for them. At best the researcher can provide insights and new perspectives by incongruity, and suggest new things to notice, reflect on, and do. If research of any kind, but especially that which is so involved in face-to-face interaction, is to be effective, then it must be articulated in terms that are meaningful in the school and community contexts. This is the case because, in the final analysis, the understanding and action of the people at the local level, who participate in practical, concrete educational circumstances, not researchers who come and go, will determine whether research results are implemented.

In sum, providing people with prearranged packages of information is oppressive, for it fails to treat people as responsible for their own lives. Furthermore, these imposed programs often have little to do with the participants' own preoccupations and practical circumstances. Providing people with ways of looking, on the other hand, reminds the participants that they are capable of acting on the world, and that these actions can transform the world. Hymes (1972: xxxvii), paraphrasing Vico together with Marx, captured this sentiment exactly: "What people have made they can understand; what people have made, people can change."

NOTES

2. The Structure of Classroom Lessons

1. Sinclair and Coulthard (1975) have also employed the concepts of initiation, directive, and elicitation in their analysis of classroom discourse. The relationship between their system of analysis and the one employed here will be explored in chapter 5.

2. A number of symbols appear in the transcripts in this and the following chapters: // is an interruption; . . . is a trailed off utterance; [is a simultaneous utterance; ( ) is nonverbal behavior; ____: is an unidentified speaker; T:_____ is an unidentifiable utterance.

3. Guilford (1956), Bloom et al. (1956) and Brophy and Good (1974) have employed similar concepts in descriptions of classroom questions. The similarities and differences between these modes of analysis will be explored in chapter 5.

3. The Structuring of Classroom Lessons

1. One instance (4:96) contained unrecorded student talk in reply to the teacher's initiation after a nominated student's reply. Two instances (4:91 and 9:29), although coded as an individual nomination and an invitation to bid, respectively, contained mixed signals about the turn-allocation procedure in effect on these occasions. One instance (4:103-105) initially seemed to be a violation of the individual nomination procedure. However, if seen as an acceptance of Alberto's delayed response by the teacher after Edward was nominated, but before he replied, this becomes a normal form of interaction.

2. Analysis of violations of the invitation to bid procedure is complicated by the ambiguity of the force of the teacher's utterance. This elicitation act, and the other unsanctioned violations of the invitation to bid procedure, contain signals instructing students to both bid for the floor and reply directly. That is, the teacher says both "who knows" and "what is this" in the same elicitation act. It is interesting to note that students reply directly *and* bid for the floor when the teacher initiates acts with these mixed signals (see 3:5, 9:29). This ambiguity of the teacher's initiation act contributes, perhaps, to the violation of these procedures.

3. The following chart shows the improvisational strategies used by the teacher by turn-allocation procedure.

Teacher's Strategies	IN	IB	IR	Total
1. The work of doing nothing	4:103			
	4:114			
a. B replies before A; T Ø	4:136			
	7:7			
B's reply is correct	9:70			
	6			3
b. B replies after A; T Ø B, T + A	4:54			
	4:99			
B's reply is correct	8:111			
c. Ss reply before T completes				
elicitation; TØ			8:23	
			8:30	
d. A replies instead of bids; T Ø;				
reply is incorrect		3:5	4:94	12
2. Getting through				
a. B replies before A, B is				
correct, T+	5:27			
	5:28			
b. A replies instead of bids; reply				
is correct; T+		5:79		
c. B replies after A; A is				
incorrect; B is correct; T +	4:135			3
3. Opening the floor				
a. After A replies incorrectly,				
B replies correctly; T +	8:125			
	8:132			
	9:79			3
4. Accepting the unexpected (an				
exception reply)	4:101			
	9:3			
	9:44			3
5. Making room	4:97			
	3:42			
	3:44			2
6. Closing out			3:10	
			3:30	2
Unanalyzed cases: 4:91, 4:96, 4:103,				
9:29				4
Total				29

4. Competent Membership in the Classroom Community

1. Many sociolinguists take umbrage at the distinction between linguistics and sociolinguistics, saying that the study of language in its social context *is* linguistics, and that the study of the formal aspects of language is but one aspect of that study (see especially Labov, 1972:181-260).

2. This example illustrates the difficulty in displaying tying structures in transcript form. Although the teacher's talk in the evaluation column of

3:34 chronologically follows Jerome's talk in the initiation column of 3:34, it does not *conversationally* follow this talk. Jerome's informative is essentially an insertion in the teacher's sequence.

3. See also 3:12-14, 3:23-24; 5:35-37; 4:58-59, 4:109-113; 5:40-42; 5:48-49; 5:53; 7:19-21; and 7:22-26; in Mehan et al., 1976.

5. Conclusions

1. Chomsky's position, at least on this point, is very similar to Hymes's (1972:xv): "Both inquiry and application are processes that involve mutuality and sharing of knowledge; neither can succeed as a one way application of *a priori* knowledge. This standpoint is one that . . . is familar to linguists and ethnographers engaged in basic research on the structure of language. Their task can be described as that of making explicit and objectively systematic what speakers of the language or members of the community, in a sense, already know."

2. For work, other than this book, generated from this project, see Cazden (1977), Cazden et al. (1978), Fisher (1976), Mehan (1977a, 1977b), Mehan et al. (1976), and Streeck (1978). Representative work from the Erickson group includes Bremme and Erickson (1977), Erickson and Shultz (1977, 1978), Florio (1978) and Shultz (1976). The work on the acquisition of functional language done at the Center for Applied Linguistics is available in Shuy and Griffin (1978). Work representative of the work on classroom interaction conducted by the Rockefeller group includes Cole, Hood, and McDermott (1978); Hall et al. (1977); McDermott (1976); McDermott and Aron (1978); McDermott, Gospodinoff, and Aron (1978).

3. Constructed by Jürgen Streeck from the GUS data (Cicourel et al., 1974:131-42).

4. I am indebted to Peg Griffin, who made this distinction clear to me.

REFERENCES

Agar, Michael
   1975 "Cognition and Events." In Mary Saches and Ben G. Blount, eds., *Sociocultural Dimensions of Language Use.* New York: Adademic Press.
Amidon, Edmund J., and Ned Flanders
   1963 *The Role of the Teacher in the Classroom.* Minneapolis: Paul S. Amidon Associates.
Austin, J. L.
   1962 *Philosophical Papers.* London: Oxford.
Bales, R. Freed
   1950 *Interaction Process Analysis.* Cambridge, Mass.: Addison Wesley.
Bauman, Richard, and Joel Sherzer
   1974 *Explorations in the Ethnography of Speaking.* New York: Cambridge University Press.
Bellack, Arno A., et al.
   1966 *The Language of the Classroom.* New York: Teachers College Press, Columbia University.
Bereiter, Karl, and Siegfried Engleman
   1972 *Teaching the Disadvantaged Child in the Preschool.* Englewood Cliffs, N.J.: Prentice-Hall.
Bernstein, Basil
   1973 *Class, Codes, and Control.* Vol. 3: *Towards a Theory of Educational Transmissions.* London: Routledge and Kegan Paul.
Berreman, Gerald
   1972 "Bringing It All Back Home: Malaise in Anthropology." In Dell H. Hymes, ed., *Reinventing Anthropology.* New York: Random House.
Birdwhistell, Ray
   1970 *Kinesics and Context.* Philadelphia: University of Pennsylvania Press.
Black, Mary, and Duane Metzger
   1969 "Ethnographic Description and the Study of the Law." In Stephan Tyler, ed., *Cognitive Anthropology.* New York: Holt, Rinehart and Winston.

213

Blau, Peter, and O. D. Duncan
1967 *The American Occupational Structure.* New York: John Wiley.
Bloom, B. S., et al., eds.
1956 "Taxonomy of Educational Objectives." In *The Classification of Education Goals, Handbook I: Cognitive Domain.* New York: David McKay.
Bowles, Samuel, and Herbert Gintes
1976 *Schooling in Capitalist America.* New York: Basic Books.
Bremme, Donald W., and Frederick Erickson
1977 "Relationships among Verbal and Nonverbal Classroom Behaviors." *Theory into Practice* 5, no. 3:153-161.
Brophy, Jere E., and Thomas L. Good
1974 *Teacher-Student Relationships: Causes and Consequences.* New York: Holt, Rinehart and Winston.
Brown, Roger
1973 *A First Language: The Early Stages.* Cambridge, Mass.: Harvard University Press.
Burnett, Jacquetta
1969 "Event Description and Analysis in the Microethnography of Urban Classrooms." In Francis Iann and E. Starey, eds., *Cultural Relevance and Educational Issues.* Boston: Little, Brown.
Byers, Paul, and Happie Byers
1972 "Nonverbal Communication and the Education of Children." In Courtney B. Cazden, Vera P. John, and Dell Hymes, eds., *Functions of Language in the Classroom.* New York: Teachers College Press.
Campbell, Donald J., and Donald W. Fiske
1959 "Convergent and Discriminant Validation by the Multitrait-Multimethod Matrix," *Psychological Bulletin* 56, no. 2:81-105.
Carrasco, R. L., A. Vera, and C. B. Cazden
In Press "Aspects of Bilingual Students' Communicative Competence in the Classroom: A Case Study." In R. Duran, ed., *Latino Language and Communicative Behavior. Discourse Processes: Advances in Research and Theory*, vol. 4. Norwood, N.J.: Ablex Publications.
Cazden, Courtney B.
1972 *Child Language and Education.* New York: Holt, Rinehart and Winston.
1976 "How Knowledge about Language Helps the Classroom Teacher, or Does It: A Personal Account." *The Urban Review* 9:74-90.
1977 "Students as Teachers." Paper presented at 1977 American Educational Research Association Convention, New York City, April 15.
Cazden, Courtney B., Vera P. John, and Dell Hymes, eds.
1972 *Functions of Language in the Classroom.* New York: Teachers College Press.
Cazden, Courtney B., et al.
1978 " 'You All Gonna Hafa Listen': Peer Teaching in a Primary Classroom." In W. A. Collins, ed., *Children's Language and Communication.* Hillsboro, N.J.: Lawrence Erlbaum.

Chomsky, Noam
   1957   "Review of Skinner." *Language* 35:26-58.
   1965   *Aspects of the Theory of Syntax*. Cambridge, Mass.: The MIT Press.
Cicourel, Aaron V.
   1964   *Method and Measurement in Sociology*. New York: The Free Press.
   1968   *The Social Organization of Juvenile Justice*. New York: Wiley.
   1973   *Cognitive Sociology: Language and Meaning in Social Interaction*. London: Penguin.
   1975   *Theory and Method in a Study of Argentine Fertility*. New York: Wiley Interscience.
Cicourel, Aaron V., and John I. Kitsuse
   1963   *Educational Decision Making*. Indianapolis: Bobbs-Merrill.
Cicourel, Aaron V., et al.
   1974   *Language Use and School Performance*. New York: Academic Press.
Clement, Dorothy C.
   1977   "Social Competence in a Desegregated School." Paper presented to Annual Meeting of the American Anthropological Association, Houston.
Cole, Michael, Lois Hood, and R. P. McDermott
   1978   "Ecological Niche Picking: Ecological Invalidity as an Axiom of Experimental Cognitive Psychology." Institute for Comparative Human Development, Rockefeller University.
Coleman, James S., et al.
   1966   *Equality of Educational Opportunity*. Washington, D.C.: U.S. Government Printing Office.
Davis, Murray S.
   1971   "That's Interesting!" *Philosophy of Social Science* 1:309-344.
Doyle, Walter
   1978   "Classroom Tasks and Student Abilities." In P. L. Peterson and H. S. Walberg, eds., *Conceptions of Teaching*. Berkeley: McCutcheon.
Dreeben, Robert
   1968   *On What Is Learned in School*. Reading, Mass.: Addison-Wesley.
Duncan, O. D., D. C. Featherman, and B. Duncan
   1972   *Socioeconomic Background and Achievement*. New York: Seminar Press.
Duncan, Starkey, Jr.
   1972   "Some Signals and Rules for Taking Speaking Turns in Conversation." *Journal of Personality and Social Psychology* 23:283-292.
Dunkin, Michael J., and Bruce J. Biddle
   1974   *The Study of Teaching*. New York: Holt, Rinehart and Winston.
Durkheim, Emile
   1896 (1938)   *The Rules of Sociological Method*. Chicago: University of Chicago Press.
   1961   *Moral Education*. New York: The Free Press of Glencoe.

Erickson, Frederick
   1975   "Gatekeeping and the Melting Pot: Interaction in Counseling
   Encounters." *Harvard Educational Review* 45:44-70.
Erickson, Frederick, and Jeffrey Shultz
   1977   "When Is a Context?" *ICHD Newsletter* 1, no. 2:5-10.
   1978   *Talking to the Man: Social and Cultural Organization of Communication in Counseling Interviews.* New York: Academic Press.
Ervin-Tripp, Susan
   1972   *Language Acquisition and Communicative Choice.* Palo Alto:
   Stanford University Press.
   1976   "Is Sybil There? The Structure of American English Directives."
   Language in Society 5:27-76.
   Ervin-Tripp, Susan, and Claudia Mitchell-Kernan
   1977   *Child Discourse.* New York: Academic Press.
Fisher, Sue
   1976   "Displaying Children's Reasoning." Paper presented to American
   Educational Research Association Meetings, San Francisco.
Flanders, N. A.
   1970   *Analyzing Teacher Behavior.* Reading, Mass.: Addison-Wesley.
Florio, Susan
   1978   "Learning How to Go to School." Ph.D. dissertation, Harvard
   University.
Florio, Susan, and Martha Walsh
   1976   "Teacher as Collaborator in Research." Paper presented at the
   1976 American Educational Research Association Convention, San
   Francisco.
Frake, Charles
   1964   "A Structural Description of Subanun Religious Behavior." In
   Ward Goodenough ed., *Explorations in Cultural Anthropology.* New
   York: McGraw-Hill.
   1969   "Notes on Queries in Anthropology." In Stephan Tyler, ed.,
   Cognitive Anthropology. New York: Holt, Rinehart and Winston.
   1977   "Plying Frames Can Be Dangerous." *ICHD Newsletter* 1, no. 3:
   1-5.
Freire, Paolo
   1968   *Pedagogy of the Oppressed.* New York: Herder and Herder.
Garfinkel, Harold
   1963   "A Conception of and Experiments with 'Trust' as a Condition of
   Concerted Stable Actions." In O. J. Harvey, ed., *Motivation and Social
   Interaction.* New York: Ronald Press.
   1967   *Studies in Ethnomethodology.* New York: Prentice-Hall.
Garfinkel, Harold, and Harvey Sacks
   1970   "The Formal Properties of Practical Actions." In John C. McKin-
   ney and Edward Tiryakian, eds., *Theoretical Sociology.* New York:
   Appleton-Century-Crofts.
Goffman, Erving
   1961   *Encounters.* Indianapolis: Bobbs-Merrill.
   1975   "Replies and Responses." *Centro Internazionale di Semiotica e*

di Linguistica 46-47:1-42.

Goodenough, Ward

1964 "Cultural Anthropology and Linguistics." In Dell Hymes, ed., *Language in Culture and Society*. New York: Harper and Row.

1976 "Multiculturalism as the Normal Human Experience." *Anthropology and Education Quarterly* 7, no. 4:4-6.

Gouldner, Alvin

1964 "Sociologist as Partisan." *American Sociologist* 3:103-116.

Griffin, Peg, and Frank Humphrey

1978 "Task and Talk." In Roger Shuy and Peg Griffin, eds., *The Study of Children's Functional Language and Education in the Early Years*. Final Report to the Carnegie Corporation of New York. Arlington, Va.: Center for Applied Linguistics.

Guilford, J. P.

1956 "The Structure of Intellect." *Psychological Bulletin* 53:267-293.

Gumperz, John J.

1964 "Linguistic and Social Interaction in Two Communities." *American Anthropologist* 66, part 2:137-153.

1971 *Language in Social Groups*. Stanford: Stanford University Press.

1976 "Language, Communication, and Public Negotiation." In P. R. Sanday, ed., *Anthropology and the Public Interest*. New York: Academic Press.

Gumperz, John J., and Dell Hymes, eds.

1964 "The Ethnography of Communication." *American Anthropologist* 66, no. 6, part 2.

Hall, William S., et al.

1977 "Variations in Young Children's Use of Language: Some Effects of Setting and Dialect." In Roy Freedle, ed., *Discourse Production and Comprehension*. Norwood, N.J.: Ablex Publishing Corporation.

Herrnstein, R. J.

1971 *I.Q. in the Meritocracy*. Boston: Little, Brown.

Hymes, Dell H.

1972 "Introduction." In Courtney B. Cazden, Vera P. John, and Dell Hymes, eds., *Functions of Language in the Classroom*. New York: Teachers College Press.

1974 *Foundations in Sociolinguistics*. Philadelphia: University of Pennsylvania Press.

Jackson, Phillip

1968 *Life in Classrooms*. New York: Holt, Rinehart and Winston.

Jencks, Christopher, et al.

1972 *Inequality*. New York: Basic Books.

Jensen, A. R.

1969 "How Much Can We Boost I.Q. and Scholastic Achievement?" *Harvard Educational Review* 39, no. 1:1-123.

Karabel, Jerome, and A. H. Halsey

1976 "The New Sociology of Education." *Theory and Society* 3:529-552.

Kendon, Adam

1970 "Movement Co-ordination in Social Interaction." *Psychologica* 32:100-124.

Labov, William
1972 *Sociolinguistic Patterns*. Philadelphia: University of Pennsylvania Press.

Labov, William, and David Fanschel
1977 *Therapeutic Discourse: Psychotherapy as Conversation*. New York: Academic Press.

Lave, Jean
1977 "Tailor Made Experiments and Evaluating the Cognitive Consequences of Apprenticeship Training." *ICHD Newsletter* 1, no. 2:1-3.

Lazersfeld, Paul F., and Morris Rosenberg
1964 *The Language of Social Research*. New York: The Free Press.

Levin, Paula
1977 "Students and Teachers: A Cultural Analysis of Polynesian Classroom Interaction." Ph.D. dissertation, University of California at San Diego.

Lewis, David
1969 *Convention*. Cambridge, Mass.: Harvard University Press.

Lewis, Michael, and Leonard Rosenblum, eds.
1977 *Interaction, Conversation, and the Development of Language*. New York: Wiley-Interscience.

McDermott, R. P.
1976 "Kids Make Sense." Ph.D. dissertation, Stanford University.

McDermott, R. P., and Jeffrey Aron
1977 "Pirandello in the Classroom." In M. Reynolds, ed., *The Futures of Education for Exceptional Students*. Reston, Va.: Council for Exceptional Children.

McDermott, R. P., and Kenneth Gospodinoff
1979 "Social Contexts for Ethnic Borders and School Failure." In A. Wolfgang, ed., *Nonverbal Behavior*. Toronto: Ontario Institute for the Study of Education.

McDermott, R. P., Kenneth Gospodinoff, and Jeffrey Aron
1978 "Criteria for an Ethnographically Adequate Description of Concerted Activities and Their Contexts." *Semiotica* 24:00-00.

Mayeske, George W.
1973 *A Study of Our Nation's Schools*. Washington, D.C.: U.S. Department of Health, Education, and Welfare.

Mead, George Herbert
1934 *Mind, Self and Society*. Chicago: University of Chicago Press.

Mehan, Hugh
1973 "Assessing Children's Language Using Abilities." In J. Michael Armer and Allen D. Grimshaw, eds., *Methodological Issues in Comparative Sociological Research*. New York: John Wiley and Sons.
1974a "Accomplishing Classroom Lessons." In A. V. Cicourel et al., *Language Use and School Performance*. New York: Academic Press.
1974b "Ethnomethodology and Education." In David O'Shea, ed.,

Sociology of the School and Schooling. Washington, D.C.: National Institute of Education.
1977a "Students' Formulating Practices and Instructional Strategies." *Annals of the New York Academy of Sciences* 285:451-476.
1977b "The Competent Student." Paper presented at the 1977 Sociology of Education Annual Meetings, San Diego.
Mehan, Hugh, and Houston Wood
1975 *The Reality of Ethnomethodology*. New York: Wiley Interscience.
1976 "De-Secting Ethnomethodology." *The American Sociologist* 11:13-21.
Mehan, Hugh, et al.
1976 "Texts of Classroom Discourse." Report no. 67a, Center for Human Information Processing, University of California at San Diego, La Jolla, California.
Merritt, Marilyn
1977 "On Questions Following Questions." *Language in Society* 5:315-358.
Mills, C. Wright
1940 "Situated Actions and Vocabularies of Movies." *American Sociological Review* 5, no. 6:904-13.
Mishler, E. G.
1975a "Studies in Dialogue and Discourse: An Exponential Law of Successive Questioning." *Language in Society* 4:31-52.
1975b "Studies in Dialogue and Discourse II: Types of Discourse Initiated by and Sustained through Questioning." *Research Journal* 4:99-121.
Moerman, Michael
1969 *A Little Knowledge*. In Stephan Tyler, ed., *Cognitive Anthropology*. New York: Holt, Rinehart and Winston.
O'Malley, J. Michael
1977 "Research Perspectives on Social Competence." *Merrill-Palmer Quarterly* 23, no. 1:29-44.
Parsons, Talcott
1937 *The Structure of Social Action*. New York: The Free Press.
1959 "The School as a Social System." *Harvard Educational Review* 29:297-318.
Philips, Susan
1972 "Participant Structures and Communicative Competence." In Courtney B. Cazden, Vera P. John, and Dell Hymes, eds., *Functions of Language in the Classroom*. New York: Teachers College Press.
1974 "The Hidden Culture." Ph.D. dissertation, University of Pennsylvania.
1976 "Some Sources of Cultural Variables in the Regulation of Talk." *Language in Society* 5:81-96.
Piaget, Jean
1970 *Main Trends in Psychology*. New York: Harper and Row.

Polanyi, Michael
   1962   *The Tacit Dimension*. New York: Harper and Row.
Pollner, Melvin
   1975   "Sociological and Common Sense Models of the Labelling Process." In Roy Turner, ed., *Ethnomethodology*. London: Penguin.
Ramos, Reyes
   1973a "The Production of Social Reality." Ph.D. dissertation, University of Colorado.
   1973b "A Case in Point." *Social Science Quarterly* 53:905-919.
Redfield, Robert
   1943   "Culture and Education in the Midwestern Highlands of Guatemala." *American Journal of Sociology* 45:640-648.
Rist, Ray L.
   1970   "Student Social Class and Teacher Expectations: The Self-Fulfilling Prophecy in Ghetto Education." *Harvard Educational Review* 40: 411-451.
Robinson, W. S.
   1951   "The Logical Structure of Analytic Induction." *American Sociological Review* 16:812-818.
Rosenbaum, James
   1976   *Making Inequality*. New York: Wiley-Interscience.
Sacks, Harvey
   1963   "Sociological Description." *Berkeley Journal of Sociology* 8:1-17.
   1973   "On The Analyzability of Stories by Children." In J. J. Gumperz and Dell Hymes, eds., *Directives in Sociolinguistics*. New York: Holt, Rinehart and Winston.
Sacks, Harvey, Emmanuel Schegloff, and Gail Jefferson
   1974   "A Simplist Systematics for the Organization of Turn-Taking in Conversation." *Language* 50:696-735.
Sanches, Mary, and Ben G. Blount
   1975   *Sociocultural Dimensions of Language Use*. New York: Academic Press.
Scheflen, Albert E.
   1972   *Communicational Structure*. Bloomington: Indiana University Press.
Schegloff, Emmanuel
   1968   "Sequencing in Conversational Openings." *American Anthropologist* 70:1075-1095.
   1972   "Notes on a Conversational Practice: Formulating Place." In David Sudnow, ed., *Studies in Interaction*. New York: The Free Press.
Schutz, Alfred
   1962   *Collected Papers*. Vol. 1. *The Problem of Social Reality*. The Hague: Martinus Nijhoff.
Searle, John
   1969   *Speech Acts*. Cambridge: Cambridge University Press.

1976 "The Classification of Illocutionary Acts." *Language in Society* 5:1-24.

Sebeok, Thomas A.
1962 "Coding in the Evolution of Signalling Behavior." *Behavioral Science* 7, no. 4:430-442.

Sewell, W. H., A. Haller, and A. Portes
1969 "The Educational and Early Occupational Attainment Process." *American Sociological Review* 34:82-92.

Shultz, Jeff
1976 "It's Not Whether You Win or Lose, But How You Play the Game." Working Paper no. 1, Newton Classroom Interaction Project, Harvard Graduate School of Education.

Shumsky, Marshall, and Hugh Mehan
1974 "The Comparability Practice of Description in Two Evaluative Contexts." Paper presented at Eighth World Congress of Sociology, Toronto.

Shuy, Roger W., and Peg Griffin, eds.
1978 *The Study of Children's Functional Language and Education in the Early Years.* Final Report to the Carnegie Corporation of New York. Arlington, Va.: Center for Applied Linguistics.

Shuy, Roger W., Walter Wolfram, and W. K. Riley
1967 *Field Techniques for an Urban Language Study.* Washington, D.C.: Center for Applied Linguistics.

Sinclair, J. M., and R. M. Coulthard
1975 *Toward an Analysis of Discourse.* New York: Oxford University Press.

Smith, Louis, and W. Geoffrey
1968 *Complexities of an Urban Classroom.* New York: Holt, Rinehart and Winston.

Snow, C. E., and C. E. Ferguson, eds.
1977 *Talking to Children.* Cambridge: Cambridge University Press.

Streeck, Jürgen
1978 "The Architecture of Conversation: Some Reasons and Revisions of Speech Act Theory." Unpublished paper, University of California at San Diego.

Sturdevant, W. C.
1964 "Studies in Ethnoscience." *American Anthropologist* 66, no. 3, part 2:99-131.

Sudnow, David
1965 *Passing On: The Social Organization of Dying.* Englewood Cliffs, N.J.: Prentice-Hall.

Sutton-Smith, Brian
1978 "Play Theory for the Rich and for the Poor." Paper presented at the Research for Better Schools/National Institute of Education Conference: Ethnography and Education, Philadelphia.

Tyler, Stephan, ed.

1969   *Cognitive Anthropology*. New York: Holt, Rinehart and Winston.
Tylor, Edward B.
1871   *Primitive Culture*. London: John Murray Publishers.
Waller, Willard
1932   *The Sociology of Teaching*. New York: John Wiley and Sons.
Warren, Richard L.
1967   *Education in Rebhausen, a German Village*. New York: Holt, Rinehart and Winston.
Weinstein, Eugene A.
1969   "The Development of Interpersonal Competence." In D. Goslin, ed., *Handbook of Socialization Theory and Research*. Chicago: Rand McNally.
Wittgenstein, Ludwig
1952   *Philosophical Investigations*. London: Basil Blackwell.
Wolcott, Harry F.
1973   *The Man in the Principal's Office*. New York: Holt, Rinehart and Winston.
Wylie, Laurence
1957   *Village in the Vaucluse*. Cambridge: Harvard University Press.
Znaniecki, Florian
1934   *The Method of Sociology*. New York: Farrar and Rinehart.

INDEX